AUTHENTIC

PARENTING

POWER

Sandi Schwartz, M.A.

In collaboration with Melissa Schwartz

You are less powerful than you want to be and more powerful than you realize.

Understanding this paradox will transform your relationship with your children.

ISBN-13: 978-1492168249

1st edition, August 2013

DEDICATION

To the children who live with us and within us, and to the power of love as a life-force that connects our hearts and souls from one generation to the next.

To my family and friends, who continually challenge and support me in living what I teach. My perseverance comes from you believing in me.

And to our first grandchild, who is on his way — May your life be filled with joy.

ACKNOWLEDGMENTS

My heart is filled with appreciation for the people who encouraged me, kept me focused, and contributed to the birthing of this book.

To my co-author, my daughter, Melissa. Without you, this book would not have been written. Your voice is a constant presence on every page.

To my husband, Steven. You are the wind beneath my wings. Your quiet strength and open arms were my refuge on the days when I was inclined to give up.

To my son, Matthew. You took me by the hand many years ago and helped me create Leading Edge Parenting, LLC. You reminded me that I could still take care of hearts while taking care of business.

To my dear friend and honored colleague, Lainie Goldstein. I treasure your friendship and the weekly dinner meetings that lasted into closing hours. Our conversations inspired, clarified, and defined my message.

To my editor, David Robert Ord. Your gift and your genius allowed me to finally stop writing. I am forever grateful for your ability to transform 300 pages that needed much organization into a brilliant manuscript.

To the parents who have trusted me with their children, their personal stories, hopes, fears, challenges and triumphs. Together we are supporting each other to live a more conscious understanding of unconditional parental love.

To the children of the Universe — and we are all little children who have just woven bigger bodies around ourselves. I honor your determination and courage to live with joyful integrity.

And to Patti, my Angel.

CONTENTS

INTRODUCTION

Behavior Begins With How a Child Feels About Themselves 2
Parenting is a Partnership 4
Loving Our Children is Only the Starting Point 6
Don't Look for Quick Fixes 9
"Welcome, Generation of Little Rebels" 11
What is Authentic Parenting? 13

CHAPTER 1
THE KEY TO UNDERSTANDING BEHAVIOR

Hardwiring 19
Children Don't Fit a Mold 21
Respect Your Child's Temperament 23
Understanding Temperament Instead of Criticizing 26

CHAPTER 2
HOW TO RECOGNIZE AND RESPOND TO YOUR CHILD'S SPECIFIC TEMPERAMENT

"Why Can't You Sit Still Like Everyone Else?"
Some Children Are Naturally More Active Than Others 30

"It's Time to Eat, So Eat"
Children Are on Their Own Bodily Schedule 32

"The World isn't Going to Change for You, So Get Used to It"
How Readily Does Your Child Adapt to Change? 34

"Get in There and Make Me Proud"
Children Handle New Situations Differently 37

"You're Too Sensitive for Your Own Good"
Things Bother Some Children That Don't Bother Others 40

"Again? What's Wrong with You?"
Every Child Feels Things Differently 43

"Stop Daydreaming and Focus"
How Easily is Your Child Distracted? 47

"How Many Times Do I Have to Tell You the Answer is 'No'?"
The Child Who Just Never Gives Up 49

Have You Come to Terms with Your Own Unique Temperament? 52

CHAPTER 3

AGES AND STAGES

Developmental Stages 59
What to Expect at Different Ages 62
Change Your "War Stories" 69

CHAPTER 4

CREATE HABITS OF EXCELLENCE

Deliberate Parenting 73
Time to Reevaluate Discipline 75
Create Guidelines That Foster Well-Being 77
Learn to Identify Teachable Moments 78
How to Handle the Challenge of Siblings 80

CHAPTER 5

EXAMINE YOUR BELIEFS ABOUT PARENTING

What are Your Core Beliefs? 87
The Part Your Subconscious Plays in Parenting 89
Release Your Past Programming 94

CHAPTER 6

AUTHENTIC PARENTING BEGINS WITH BEING HONEST WITH YOURSELF

A Sense of Self 101
Come Out from Behind Your Mask 103
Why You Should Engage in Self-Reflection 104
How to Deliberately Shift Your Thoughts 107
Limiting Thoughts 109
Empowering Thoughts 109
How Shifting Your Thoughts Works in Practice 112

CHAPTER 7

THE ANSWERS LIE IN YOUR BRAIN

Beliefs Create Pathways 119
Master Your Own Mind 120
How to Change Your Brain Patterns 124
Your Primitive Brain 126
Don't Mistake Fear for Love 128
How to Influence Your Child's Brain Development 130
Implications for Parenting 133
The Importance of Staying Positive 136

CHAPTER 8
HOW EMOTIONS FUEL BEHAVIOR

Notice Your Triggers 141
What's the Emotion Behind the Behavior? 142

CHAPTER 9
HOW TO PARENT EFFECTIVELY DESPITE YOUR OWN CHILDHOOD WOUNDS

Uncovering Your Wounds 149
Giving Up Worry 151

CHAPTER 10
WAYS WE TRY TO CONTROL A CHILD'S FEELINGS

Emotional Enmeshment 157
The Fixer 159
The Lecturer 160
The Nag 160
The Guilt Tripper 160
The Shamer 161
The Sergeant 162
The Bully 162
The Intimidator 163
The Abuser 164

CHAPTER 11
DEVELOP EMOTIONAL RESILIENCE

Emotional Health Begins With Meeting Needs 169
How to Meet Your Child's Bodily Needs 170
The Importance of Physical and Emotional Safety 172
Foster a Sense of Belonging 174
Become a Coach for Your Children 177
Negative Emotions Mean Something Needs to Change in Us 178
There's Legitimacy in that Behavior 180
Acknowledge Your Child's Feelings 185
Forget About "Yes, But..." 188

CHAPTER 12
HELP YOUR CHILDREN DISCOVER THEIR INNER GUIDANCE SYSTEM

Self Awareness 195
Blaming Others for Our Behavior 198
Listening for Inner Guidance 200
Encouraging Children to Use Their Own GPS 202
We Teach What We Live 203
A Gift To Our Children 206

CHAPTER 13
TAP INTO YOUR PARENTING POWER

Everything is Energy 211
The Importance of Surrendering to Energy 212
How to Attract What You Want 215
A Daily Tune-up 217

CONCLUSION

Our Soul's Journey 223
Passion and Purpose 224
Give Up Control 226
An Era of Shifting Energy 228
10 Best Practices for Parents 232

INTRODUCTION

My work with families has shown me that even the most intelligent, successful, and aware adults struggle when it comes to parenting. The reason for this is that parenting involves the art of managing both our power and our powerlessness.

Each of us is less powerful than we want to be and more powerful than we realize. To accept this paradox is the key to transforming our relationship with our children.

There's so much we can do — and simultaneously so little we can do. The trick is to do what we can well. This we accomplish when we clear the way for the power inherent in our love to flow freely.

So why wouldn't love flow freely? After all, from the moment our children enter the world, every fiber of our parental nature pulses with a longing for them to be safe, happy, and successful.

We can compare parenting as humans to Mother Earth herself. Nature is simultaneously a source of vital sustenance and capable of great destruction. Consequently all of life exists on a knife-edge. For instance, simply by dropping showers from clouds blown in from the ocean, earth has the ability to nurture a seedling into a magnificent tree. Yet the same wind that bears on its wings life-giving moisture can become a whirling storm dumping torrential downpours able to uproot even a giant oak.

In parenting, as in much of life, there's a fine line between caring and controlling. When we care, we draw out a child's inherent goodness; whereas when we control, we invite dysfunction.

It's widely believed that parents are supposed to control their children. Many of us were brought up to believe it's the parent's job to discipline their children to get them to fall in line. However, research into the effects of discipline, borne out by my extensive practical experience as a child development specialist, reveals that controlling children not only leads to frustration for the parents but is one of the primary causes of distress and misbehavior in children.

The problem is that whereas caring nurtures, control can wreak havoc with a child's sense of well-being. The repercussions of damaging a child's self-esteem then reverberate through every area of their lives, affecting not only the rest of the family but also the wider society in which they must function on a daily basis.

BEHAVIOR BEGINS WITH HOW A CHILD FEELS ABOUT THEMSELVES

Although as a culture we've been deluged with information about how to bring up children, it's still not commonly recognized that *a child's behavior is an expression of how they feel about themselves*. We don't seem to realize that we can never raise emotionally healthy human beings if we damage their inherent sense of well-being.

If our children's lives are to be responsible, productive, and fulfilling, the desire for this has to come from a different source than our attempts at control. It has to flow out of a child's own center — out of *how they see themselves and feel about themselves*.

We so easily create a web of confusion for our children, entangling their innocent spirit, by insisting they see things from *our* viewpoint. Controlling them in this way, they lose touch with their own center — and herein lies the source of just about all the behavioral problems we encounter. It's hard to live a fantastic life when you feel anything but fantastic inside yourself.

Many parents have told me over the years that they have a right to raise their children as they see fit. This is why it's so common to hear a parent declare, "Don't tell me how to raise my child." I understand why parents feel this way: it's because they naturally assume they have their child's best interests more at heart than anyone else. However, because in many cases we are so invested in our children in terms of what they mean for our *own* sense of self-identity, the line between encouraging and controlling, nurturing and suffocating, and being openhearted and indulgent is so fine that we are ever prone to get it wrong.

Unhealthy expressions of parental power shows up as coercion, manipulation, and putting pressure on children. Equally harmful is the behavior of a parent who is disconnected, unaware, or too distracted to create structure or establish appropriate limits and boundaries within a framework of unconditional love. Both approaches are damaging. For effective parenting, the goal has to be a balance of freedom within sensible limits.

To state that control is detrimental to children doesn't mean we don't teach our children. Teaching a child is fundamentally different from controlling them. It's a parent's job to encourage habits of excellence. However, a child's brain doesn't develop positive patterns from parental yelling, threatening, punishing, or dismissing, which are actually expressions of control.

On the contrary, the way we express our own emotions, handle family relationships and respond to daily challenges are what influence the way our children cope with life more than anything we tell them to do. When we model self-respect, integrity, and effective conflict resolution, our children learn from watching us.

The paradox of parenting power is that as soon as we give up needing to be in control and shift our focus to understanding our child's needs, answers to baffling situations begin to flow. Once we taste the freedom of letting go of what we can't ever truly control, we become open to the wisdom and intuition that gives us real power.

PARENTING IS A PARTNERSHIP

Parents are pressured to produce children who are reflections of the social norms. Many parents imagine they are creating a nurturing environment because their children appear successful by society's standards. I argue that our greatness begins when we stop caring what others think and decide in our heart what type of parent we really want to be, together with the kind of home environment we want our children to grow up in. Creating the vision we want for our family may require challenging the status quo and facing resistance from people who are stuck in outmoded thinking.

Although we can't control the impact of peer pressure and the social media, what goes on inside the privacy of our homes ultimately has the greatest influence on our children's attitudes and behavior. Coming into our power as parents enables us to see that success in terms of our children involves how they feel on the inside rather than how they appear to the external world. An empowered parent is courageous enough to care less about what other people think, instead being concerned about what works for their child's particular cosmic design.

When I speak of "cosmic design," I think of this as the unique combination of physical, mental, emotional, and spiritual hardwiring that constitutes each individual. It includes our essence, our genes, and the combined impact of our relationships, environment, and experiences — in other words, everything that gives us our distinctive makeup. Elsewhere, I refer to this as our particular "blueprint."

Our children's worthiness to live a life of inspiration in which they express themselves, appreciate each moment, and reach for their potential based on their specific cosmic design, is their birthright. Success is ultimately about living a life that's fully alive. To support such a life, the parenting task isn't to determine a child's path for them, but to recognize that each of us is on an individual yet co-creative journey toward the full expression of our uniqueness.

It may come as a surprise to hear that you and your children are ideal partners for this journey. If you accept that you are here not to exert control but to learn from each other, you'll discover that you can translate every challenge into an opportunity for the expansion of your true self — with the spinoff that your children also grow toward their potential.

When we decide to make a change in response to a situation that invites us to grow, our initial reaction may be resistance. I'm quite sure many will resist some of what I have to share. Be aware that doubt and fear often lurk behind our arguments against a course of action. I encourage you to be brave and unwavering in your intention to grow as you expand your understanding of the dynamics of the child-parent relationship.

Change occurs when we reach tipping points. The tipping point in parenting is that magic "aha" moment when we suddenly understand what's causing our child's behavior and our reaction to it. Tipping points are powerful because they awaken our willingness to try something different. Each chapter of this book will give you information that has the potential to trigger an "aha" moment that can nudge you over your tipping point and into something extraordinary.

Parenting brings incredible joys and equal challenges, since we are no longer accountable for just ourselves. Taking on the responsibility of raising children awakens emotions that bring forth the best and worst in us. A child's basic nature, emotional reactivity, unique spiritual journey, and connection to an ever-expanding universe are elements of a system so complex that it's no wonder parents often feel baffled and overwhelmed.

I raised two very different children during an era when my family, friends, and the "experts" had opposing ideas about which style of parenting was preferable. On really challenging days, I wished for a crystal ball — guidance with magical clout. In this book, I decode the mysteries of the parent-child relationship. The magic offered is a synthesis of investigation in the field of child development, leveraging the power of thoroughly tested research that often contradicts popular opinion, and a growing awareness that our relationship with our children is a *reflection of our relationship with ourselves*.

LOVING OUR CHILDREN IS ONLY THE STARTING POINT

When I ask my child development students why they want to be teachers, the answer they overwhelmingly give is, "Because I love children." I have no doubt this is true. But loving is only the beginning. Many people, young and old, love each other, yet they can't get along.

Why did *you* choose to become a parent? What's your vision for your family?

Most of us drift into the parenting experience without a definite sense of purpose. Remembering that love is just the beginning, your effectiveness is limited only by a willingness to expand your understanding of what parenting is really all about — and it *isn't* about getting children to be "well behaved." Love never involves controlling another human being.

For love to be effective, it can't just be a feeling we have for our children. Rather, it has to be channeled in such a way that it supports the inherent state of well-being with which our children came into the world. Think of a hydroelectric power plant. When water spreads out across a plain, you can't generate electricity. The water has to be channeled between the banks of a river. Well, love is like that. Before it can enable a child to blossom, it has to be harnessed and used with insight and wisdom.

Thinking we know what's best for our kids just because we love them has led to generations of unhappy individuals, failed or mediocre relationships, and unfulfilled dreams — not to mention social and global turmoil. Even parents with the best of intentions unwittingly muddy the waters for their children to some degree. As a result, at any given time literally millions of adults are in some kind of counseling trying to sort themselves out. Statistics on the use of antidepressants, alcohol, and drugs for children age twelve and over are a staggering indictment of the condition of our collective emotional health.

While love involves feelings and often requires us to make certain decisions, fundamentally it's a state of being. Indeed, it's our most natural state — the way we behave when we are in touch with our center, our essence, our spirit or soul. The further we move from this bedrock state, the more disconnected from ourselves we feel. To be in touch with our unconditionally loving essence is the path to empowerment — and to empowering our children.

A willingness to discover what our children need from us to foster the development of their unique being is the first step to unlocking the real parenting power of love. When parents get caught up in their own agenda, they miss opportunities to help their children develop in their own special way.

It's essential to accept that we have no control over our children's unique cosmic design, which is hardwired and powered by their soul's purpose. It affects the way they perceive and respond to their surroundings. It generates the patterns of behavior that precipitate life's lessons. As parents, our greatest contribution is to provide a safe space in which our children can learn about themselves and flourish as the never-to-be-repeated individuals they inherently are.

While we can't control our children's unique hardwiring, we can nevertheless play a real role in shaping how each child's blueprint pans out in everyday reality. How children think about themselves, develop relationships, and perceive their world depends largely on the messages they receive from us as their parents.

The ability to lovingly guide children requires a combination of our natural intuition, knowledge of the principles of child development, and being willing to look at the way our own beliefs and experiences unconsciously lead us to make typical parenting mistakes.

DON'T LOOK FOR QUICK FIXES

Many parents want an easy fix for complicated issues. They want to know how to get their children to listen or how to stop them from displaying poor behavior. However, effective parenting isn't about a quick fix. This is because parental responses to children's behavior must meet short-term needs as well as long-term goals. For this reason parenting can never be about clever techniques and tricks designed to control a child. Instead, it begins with *connecting*.

Each child has a unique makeup with particular needs. The parent's task is to connect with the uniqueness of their children. Since what a child really needs is often so different from what we imagine — and different from those of our other children and other people's children — there can never be a manual for parenting. We are all too complicated to reduce our experiences to a singular operating system.

Understanding why a particular child behaves the way they do, and how our approach either encourages or shuts down their inherent state of well-being, is essential to bringing a child's best self forward.

As children move through the stages and challenges of human development, their unique makeup impacts their behavior. When we stop taking their actions personally and examine what they are triggering in our own inner world, we become empowered to respond in a manner that not only honors but capitalizes on their makeup. Having addressed the reason we react, we can now address their particular needs in a fitting way.

How this works in practice can be seen from Betsy, the mother of Julia, a stubborn and power-seeking eleven-year-old. Betsy had an "aha" moment when she realized that it was Julia's hardwiring, not outright defiance of parental authority, that made it impossible for Julia to comply with many of Betsy's demands. In order for Julia to feel more in control of her life, Betsy realized she had to allow Julia more choices for when she did her homework, what she ate for snacks, and her selection of clothes. Demanding that Julia listen to Betsy simply because "she's the mom," went against Julia's need to feel empowered and more in control of her life. Betsy realized that Julia's refusal to comply was a factor of her cosmic hardwiring exacerbated by a normal stage of development. Demanding that a child with this temperament be compliant is like requiring a table to turn itself into a chair. When Betsy allowed her daughter more choices, giving her opportunities to voice her opinions and affirming some of her suggestions, this stubborn tween became considerably more cooperative. This was a tipping point that drastically changed the energy between mother and daughter.

If we don't know a child's true needs — don't understand how they perceive their world and how they develop — we can't parent them in the way they require. We will misjudge what their behavior is really about and apply the wrong solution. This is why so many of our young people, especially when they reach their teens, prove to be a headache for parents.

When parents try to deal with power struggles without recognizing the way the human brain interprets messages, they are missing a key component in understanding what drives children's behavior. Only with understanding can we leverage our power effectively, thereby helping our children grow up true to their blueprint.

Authentic empowerment begins with accepting our children exactly as they are, which requires giving up the need to mold them according to a prescribed formula and giving up the dream of what we wish they would be. We are embarrassed when our children don't share, are uncooperative, throw a tantrum, or behave irresponsibly. We are so hooked into the thought we might be judged, we have a knee-jerk reaction that entails making demands, threatening, or punishing, rather than patiently teaching our children the skills needed to act differently.

Powerful parenting involves detaching from our ideas of how a child *should* turn out, focusing instead on nurturing our children's gifts in ways that encourage authentic self-esteem. Character is built on appreciation for the expression of realistic gifts, coupled with determination to meet challenges. When we are oblivious to, or over-inflate, our children's victories, they develop a false sense of self.

"WELCOME, GENERATION OF LITTLE REBELS"

Something is changing — can you sense it? Some say children are different than ever before. I agree: they are.

The latter part of the 20th century and the beginning of the 21st century have together ushered in an era when, unlike any other time in our species' long history, parents are challenged to keep up with their children. One of our main challenges is to wake up to a *more authentic way of being.*

Some of the children who are being born in the 21st century have more sophisticated wiring than past generations. Many of these little ones also have intuitive abilities beyond their parents' ability to comprehend. Some of them seem to be wise beyond their years.

Many of these kids refuse to be controlled by the kind of fear and guilt that ruled so many generations before them. They can sniff out inauthentic people and know when they are being manipulated. Refusing to comply with limiting and dysfunctional systems, they question anyone and challenge anything that needs changing. Young warriors, they push us to expand our consciousness in a way that shakes up our established systems. Hence it's both a blessing and a challenge to parent these children.

The beginning of the 21st century has been a challenging time for parents and teachers because we are learning how to set up environments that respect and nourish this new kind of child. Slowly, we are moving away from thinking something's wrong because these children have unique styles of interacting and don't connect in conventional ways. We are being required to evaluate afresh just what is "normal," since behavior currently labeled as ADHD and Autistic may be the forerunners of new models of thriving. What we currently judge to be "special needs" might represent sophisticated talent.

As we are forced to adapt to these sensitive souls, we have an opportunity to ask questions that can lead to real change, such as: What kind of school environment works best for this child? How should we set up limits so they can follow the beat of their own inner drum and still thrive? How might the challenges of this child awaken something great within *us*?

I said that parenting is a partnership. The new ones coming in are insisting we take an honest look at ourselves. As adults, we don't always want to look at our own behavior — we prefer to focus on the kids. We know what we want them to do: we want them to be good, responsible, caring, empathic, and polite. Our message to them is "eat your food, do your homework, play nicely, and make me proud of you." My message to you is to do your own inner work and watch the miracles unfold.

WHAT IS AUTHENTIC PARENTING?

Authentic parenting isn't about raising children who comply with society's expectations and thereby make us look good. On the contrary, we pay a high price when we find it more compelling to brag about our child's ability to potty train early, make the team, or be accepted at a prestigious school than to wonder how they feel about themselves. Children who come to believe that all their parents care about are good grades, following rules, and making them proud often become teenagers who push back, hide the truth, and in some cases shut down, develop physical ailments, get into serious trouble, or take their own life. Control backfires as young adults refuse to be over-managed.

Children are aware that parents tend to care more about how they behave than how they feel, and this awareness is creating a new kind of generation gap. The generation gap used to mean changes in music, clothing, and hairstyles. Today we are experiencing technological advancement unprecedented in the history of our species. Our children are born technology ready, enthusiastically devouring ever-changing means of communicating and connecting.

Less obvious and more confusing to parents are the energetic shifts also taking place. Our children are pushing us to look at ourselves and reevaluate many of the beliefs, values, and standards we have long regarded as unassailable "truths." They are demanding, through their behavior, that we look in the mirror, then step out of the shadows of propriety and begin to be real. Consequently they don't cave into authority as did previous generations. They are little rebels insisting we clean up our own act and grow along with them.

Our children realize we don't like being challenged to be authentic role models for them. When they hold up a mirror to our inauthenticity, we tend to get angry with them. However, if we are willing to partner in the process with them, we will discover that being pushed to give up our own hypocrisy is a gift.

Increasingly, parenting in the 21st century is more about raising the awareness of the parent than about the behavior of the child. The reason for this is that when we find our true power by giving up the antiquated and toxic beliefs about "making children behave" that haunted past generations, we change the energy with which we approach our children. The child then naturally behaves in a more cooperative, pleasant, and joyful manner.

How do I know it works this way? Because I have seen these miraculous changes take place in families and classrooms for the past forty years.

As we examine the parent-child relationship, it will be helpful to keep in mind that parents are just little kids who grew bigger bodies. Along the way, we accumulated networks of beliefs and patterns of behavior. So although as adults we occupy the parenting role, we often operate from the mindset that influenced us when we were young. Unless we consciously uncover this conditioning from our childhood there will be times when our own emotional toddler, rather than our wise adult self, will be parenting our children.

Finding the courage to be an authentic parent requires becoming aware of when we are parenting from our own emotional immaturity. As I mentioned previously, such awareness may engender discomfort as we find ourselves having to jettison some of the beliefs about parenting instilled in us by our culture, family, or friends. We each move into our role as parent with a personal thermostat of comfort in the way we interact with our children. However, changing some of our patterns of thinking and behaving will create the shift that leads us into our authentic power.

CHAPTER 1

THE KEY TO UNDERSTANDING BEHAVIOR

"What lies before us and what lies behind us are small matters compared to what lies within us. And when we bring what is within out into the world, miracles happen."

— Henry David Thoreau

HARDWIRING

The fundamental reason children act the way they do is their hardwiring. Each child is a unique creation. Consequently, once we let go of any predetermined ideas of how our children should look, behave, perform, or make us feel, we become free to experience and embrace them for the gems they are. This enables us to work *with* them, instead of constantly battling to control them.

While many of us embark on parenthood imagining we will unconditionally love each child, our attitude often changes once a child's hardwiring becomes a source of inconvenience, annoyance, disappointment, or cause for concern. When the child behaves differently from standards of "acceptability," we think it's our parental job to change the child. Because our identity is wrapped up in our child's behavior, we take their actions personally. Our sense of well-being becomes dependent on how they perform. When we expect a child to change so we can feel better, we can easily exhaust ourselves trying to change the unchangeable.

Thinking we need to control a child's behavior often leads to frustration because, no matter how much the child loves us, it's impossible for them to always be what we want them to be and simultaneously interact with the world according to their individual cosmic design. For example: If our child is a natural introvert we cannot demand that he perform like his extroverted sibling. If our child is a gifted artist he may not want to play a contact sport even if everyone else in the family expects him to do so.

This approach to parenting isn't a free for all. We don't have to tolerate outrageous behavior, save them from the consequences of their decisions or give up standards and boundary setting. A child-centered home doesn't mean turning all decisions over to the kids. Creating an environment that brings out the best in each child can only be done when we as parents take the time and make the effort to acquaint ourselves with the unique traits, strengths, and weaknesses of each child's natural wiring.

All humans are physically hardwired. The way our brain and body react to life is rooted in our fundamental makeup. In the same way we wouldn't demand a child change the color of their eyes, it's just as unreasonable to expect them to change how easily they become frustrated or how long they can sit still. As parents, we are our children's greatest teacher, which requires learning how to help them adjust to the demands of life while appreciating their individuality.

The more we understand a child's inner world, the more effectively we can respond to them. Amazingly, when a child senses they are seen for who they really are, and that we are grateful to have them in our life exactly as they are, they actually *want* to please us. We have no control over whether they are a visual, auditory, or kinesthetic learner; a natural introvert or extrovert; intuitive or analytical; athletic or creative. A wise parent creates an environment in which children are encouraged to figure out who they are, are given opportunities that amplify their natural gifts, and receive the message that their hardwiring doesn't determine their worthiness.

Once we understand a child's temperament, the next step is to examine our own. Our first "aha" moment might be when we realize our child's temperament is triggering something in us. It may be comforting to know we have no control over *anyone's* hardwiring, not even our own.

CHILDREN DON'T FIT A MOLD

When we have a predetermined idea of who our children "should" be, we rob ourselves of the opportunity to experience the fullness of each child's nature. Perhaps even more importantly, we interfere with their ability to know and appreciate themselves. We may even cause them to feel there's something inherently flawed about them. Our tendency to evaluate their behavior by some collective standard of what makes a child "good" stops us from seeing them for the masterpieces they are.

If you have a child with an easygoing temperament, you may wonder why other parents are having such a hard time. However, if you are blessed with children who have sensitive, intense, freedom-seeking circuitry, you will have a bumpier ride.

I love to tell the following story as a way of helping parents understand that these little beings arrive on our planet with their own unique way of experiencing and responding to life.

A mom gives birth to twins. We meet these children in the hospital nursery when they are two days old. They are like little angels from heaven. We know they are fraternal twins, not identical twins, because they are male and female. They come from the same mom and dad but carry a different mix of genes. Their arrival is celebrated with awe and wonder as we are introduced to these sleeping darlings. The little boy stirs. He doesn't seem to be affected by the lights or sounds in the nursery. Noticing the wet feeling in his diaper, he begins to coo and purr as if to say, "Can anyone do something about this uncomfortable feeling?" A little while later he becomes aware of the hunger in his belly and moves his little fists, crying softly, "Hurry up, please; I'm in need of attention."

When his sister awakens, the soft nursery lights feel like an attack on her sensory system, so she begins to cry vociferously. "Yikes!" she seems to be communicating. "What is this? Where am I? I don't like those lights shining in my eyes." The next moment, she feels her wet diaper, and her fists and legs struggle to get out from under her blanket. Overwhelmed by pangs of hunger, her little face contorts and reddens as her screams send the staff scurrying. When the nurse hands the baby to her mom, she comments with a mischievous smile, "Ooh, she's going to be a handful."

The judgments have begun. Even though parents say they love and accept each child exactly as the child comes into the world, the reality is that we quickly categorize the baby who lies quietly as the "good one" and the infant who fusses as the "difficult one." Naturally, it's easier to live with a child who isn't thrown off balance by everyday life. However, children who struggle need to know there's nothing wrong with them.

Each of the infants in our story perceived the same experiences differently and therefore had different reactions. The little girl deserves to grow up knowing that the way she experiences life is just as valid as her brother's experience of life; and that even though her behavior can be challenging, she is inherently loveable. The parents' responsibility isn't to demand she fit a mold, but to help her learn to soothe herself. Children who move through life with sensitive, intense, or unusual blueprints push the limits of parents' patience. It can be challenging and even frightening to live with a child whose behavior is baffling. I know this because I gave birth to children just like those in our story. Our son was born four years before our daughter. Because Matthew was an easygoing toddler who always listened, I wasn't prepared for Melissa's responses and spent the first three years of her life trying to mold her into a compliant child like her brother.

I didn't realize that Matthew's blueprint made it possible for him to handle parental requests, change, and frustration easily. I thought it was my brilliant parenting! Melissa's fundamentally different blueprinting proved to be the perfect challenge to launch my own journey into maturity. I came to see that it was I who had to change.

Before Melissa was born, I thought I knew everything I needed to know about kids. After all, I had prestigious degrees and had experienced a high level of success both as an educator and as a parent raising our son. Only with Melissa's birth did my real learning get underway.

RESPECT YOUR CHILD'S TEMPERAMENT

The bridge between intellectual understanding and parenting with unbounded love begins by making peace with the part of a child's makeup known as their temperament. This stays with a child throughout life, since it's the individual's unique way of being.

In practice this means that each child comes with a different "style." Some make peace with physical life easily, having an innate tendency to well-being that enables them to shake off challenges and go with the flow. Others seem to struggle, deeply affected by strong internal impulses as well as their environment. The best we can offer them is to learn what they need from us and respond in a supportive manner that helps them navigate their lives.

Temperament styles fall into three broad categories. No judgment is intended in these descriptions:

The at-ease child appears to handle life calmly and without too much difficulty. Such children find their rhythm and make peace with their surroundings. Parents describe them as "easy to handle" and label them "good" children because they tend to be flexible and easily adapt to different situations. Because of this tendency, it's essential for a parent not to give such children the idea that their role in life is to please others. They deserve the freedom to express their opinions and wishes without feeling they need approval.

The highly-aware child seems to notice everything — you might say they are detail-oriented. Extremely sensitive to their surroundings, huge emotional reactions are their norm. It can be challenging for a parent when a highly-aware child is uncomfortable with the way something feels, smells, or tastes. Rather than judging such children as "fussy" or "difficult," it's important to honor their intensity and help them coexist with life. If nurtured with understanding, these children can learn to soothe themselves, which frees them to use their sensitivity to have a positive impact on their world.

The taking-my-time child likes to flow with life, which requires considerable patience on the part of adults. It takes these children longer to adjust to new people and places. They may not be eager to try different foods or might resist entering an unfamiliar situation. It's a mistake to think that hurrying such children or demanding them to "get moving" is helping them feel secure. However, once a child with this temperament feels comfortable on their own, their gifts begin to emerge.

While many children's temperaments overlap traits from each of these "styles," there are specific tendencies that give us insight into how to attune ourselves to a child's needs. These traits also help us predict behavior. When parents help a child discover their nature, accepting and embracing them exactly as they are, such children are far more likely to grow up to be adults who more readily integrate their inner and outer worlds.

The reason it can be so challenging to totally accept a child is that, as parents, we have our own unique temperament. Misunderstanding and conflict arise when parents and children are hardwired in such a way they automatically push each other's buttons.

"We're both so stubborn," one parent tells me. Says another, "We're both too sensitive." On the other hand, a third parent opines, "I'm so easygoing. I don't understand why my child has to make such a big deal of everything all the time."

When we understand rather than judge these dynamics, we learn to appreciate each other's traits. We can lighten up and make peace with our own temperament, as well as with the temperament of each particular child.

UNDERSTANDING TEMPERAMENT
INSTEAD OF CRITICIZING

Temperament isn't a child's total identity but the starting place for understanding how a child experiences life and reacts to their environment. Once we become conscious of a child's temperament, we have taken the first step toward not taking their behavior personally, which is key to effective use of our parenting power.

When a child reacts, it's crucial we don't then react to them. Since we are no longer in control of our actions when we react emotionally, to react is the opposite of exercising our power. Only when we are non-reactive can we parent from a place of power.

Because we no longer feel a need to complain about or control behavior that pulses from temperament, we can release all demands for our child to change. Instead, we learn how to "be with" a child. We anticipate problems and design strategies that encourage cooperation based on each child's uniqueness.

While we may not like the challenging behavior that comes from our child's temperament, the miracles begin as soon as we change how we think about what's really going on inside of them. We can soothe ourselves, learn appropriate strategies, and approach them in a way that frees us to connect from the heart.

CHAPTER 2

HOW TO RECOGNIZE AND RESPOND TO
YOUR CHILD'S SPECIFIC TEMPERAMENT

"To be yourself in a world that is constantly trying to make
you something else is the greatest accomplishment."

— Ralph Waldo Emerson

Dr. Stella Chase and Dr. Alexander Thomas identify a number of components of temperament:

ACTIVITY LEVEL
The amount of movement or activity that seems to feel comfortable and natural for the child

REGULARITY AND RHYTHM OF BODILY ROUTINES
The ease with which the child is able to relax into daily routines such as eating, eliminating, and sleeping

ABILITY TO ADAPT TO CHANGE
The ease with which a child can deal with changes in the schedule and environment

INITIAL REACTION
How smoothly the child reacts to something new

SENSITIVITY TO THE ENVIRONMENT
Reactions to lights, noise, smells, texture, movement, energy, such as tags on back of clothes or crowds in restaurants

INTENSITY OF REACTION AND STRENGTH OF RESPONSE
The degree to which they "feel" and express their feelings

EASE OF DISTRACTION
How easily their attention is refocused by a noise, movement, or the introduction of another person in the room

PERSISTENCE AND LENGTH OF ATTENTION SPAN
How much time the child spends pursuing something wanted or focused in an activity

"WHY CAN'T YOU SIT STILL LIKE EVERYONE ELSE?"

SOME CHILDREN ARE NATURALLY MORE ACTIVE THAN OTHERS

Activity level has to do with the amount of movement that creates comfort and balance for a child. Some children need to run and jump, moving fairly constantly. Others are content to sit quietly for long periods. Picture a four-year-old sitting quietly at the kitchen table. They are still for an hour, happily coloring with a variety of art supplies as mom prepares dinner and folds the laundry. Ever since infancy, this child has been satisfied with little movement, and as a result constantly receives messages about how "good" they are.

Several years later the same parents have another child. When the second child is four years old, they can't sit quietly for more than five minutes. As an infant, they cried to be held and carried, demanding to bounce along in a sling on their father's chest. Their natural inclination is to run instead of walk.

One child feels satisfied with little movement, whereas the other child needs much more activity. Neither is being "good" or "bad," terms that we would be wise to remove from our parenting vocabulary. Our power comes from observing a child's nature, training ourselves to work with it, and giving up wishing their temperament were different.

High activity children can cause a parent to feel powerless. If you have a toddler or preschooler with a high activity level, it's important to understand that this child *must* move. To exercise appropriate parental power, you don't want to fall into the trap of trying to disconnect the generator that powers your child's body. Your power lies in accepting your child's need to move and figuring out how they can meet this need. If you provide enough time and space to run, jump, swing, ride a bike, or chase a ball, the chances are much better they will be able to walk through the house, sit still in their chair, or concentrate on an activity when such is required. It's too hard for a high-activity child to walk inside the house if they haven't had sufficient opportunity to be active in a safe place.

Yelling and punishing are ineffective because they fail to meet an active child's needs. Not only are they ineffective, but you can be laying the groundwork for a real problem if you take away a child's ability to do what by nature they must do.

The flip side of this is that a highly active parent may have plenty of energy to keep up with an active child, while being frustrated by a child who doesn't want to play ball but would rather you sit with them and do a craft project or read a book. In contrast, a low-activity parent may enjoy more laid-back fun and find keeping up with a child who can't sit still exhausting.

Again, though you can't change your active child's temperament, you can change the way you think about it. For instance, you might say to yourself, "My child is vigorous and energetic, full of life and always on the go. Their body is filled with potential to enjoy athletics and an active lifestyle." To help with this, you may wish to use the following affirmations:

I let go of the things I cannot control.

I cannot control my child's temperament. It's part of their unique cosmic design.

I release my child's active temperament and love them exactly as they are, allowing plenty of time for them to release the energy in their body. As they grow older, they will learn how to meet their need for activity for themselves.

I am a role model. I nurture my own well-being and honor my own unique temperament.

My child and I are worthy of love, exactly as we are.

My intention is to extend the love that lives inside me to everything I think about my child and myself.

You can help a highly active child by using validating statements: "It looks like you need to move before you are ready to come to the table. Can you jump up and down thirty times? I'll count for you." You can also encourage such a child to think about ways to get their body ready to come to the table. This will impart a valuable sense of self-control.

"IT'S TIME TO EAT, SO EAT"

CHILDREN ARE ON THEIR OWN BODILY SCHEDULE

Bodily rhythms regulate the consistency of a child's eating, sleeping, and eliminating patterns. It's easier for parents when their little ones can adjust to the family's eating and sleeping routines or lack thereof. When the parents' lifestyle is inconsistent, it can be quite challenging if a child needs a predictable schedule. Conversely, a child who lives in a home with rigid routines may be hardwired to function with greater flexibility.

When a child's temperament doesn't match the lifestyle we prefer, it can feel as though the child is testing us. For this reason it's important to take time to observe each child's natural rhythms. When we do so, we no longer misinterpret their struggles as a willful act of defiance. Instead we learn from their cues, which enables us to release our unrealistic beliefs about when a human body must eat, eliminate, or sleep. Mealtime and bedtime routines can then be designed to respect a child's unique wiring, avoiding the kind of frustration that easily results in a meltdown.

Again, it's important to understand how your own temperament differs from that of your child. If you have a temperament that likes routine, it can be challenging to raise a child who doesn't naturally adhere to your schedule of eating, bathing, and sleeping. In contrast, if it's easy for you to function with less structure, you may have a hard time understanding why your child can't tolerate unpredictable mealtimes and bedtimes.

Since you can't change your child's natural bodily rhythms, the challenge is to change the way you think about such matters. You might tell yourself, "My child seems to do better with consistent, predictable eating and sleeping routines." Or in the opposite case, "My child seems to do better with flexibility around eating and sleeping." To help with this, I recommend the following affirmations:

I let go of the things I cannot control.

I cannot control my child's temperament, since it's part of their unique cosmic design.

I accept my child's natural bodily rhythms and love them exactly as they are, allowing for the predictability or flexibility they need.

I let go of preconceived ideas, honor my child's needs, and create a daily pattern that works best for this child.

I am a role model for my child. I nurture my own well-being and honor my own unique temperament.

My child and I are worthy of love, exactly as we are.

My intention is to extend the love that lives inside me to everything I think about my child and myself.

You can help a child who is irregular in their patterns by saying, "It's hard for you to fall asleep. You don't have to sleep, but you must stay in your bed. What will help you?" Similarly, you might help a child who tends toward regular patterns to cope with an unpredictable day by saying, "Let's pack a snack for you, just in case lunch runs a little late."

The key is to acquaint yourself with your child's style. If they need regularity in their schedule, be mindful of timing when it comes to meals and sleep. If your child has an irregular pattern, you can encourage them to sit with the family and get into bed at prescribed times, while allowing them to actually eat and fall asleep when their body is ready.

"THE WORLD ISN'T GOING TO CHANGE FOR YOU, SO GET USED TO IT"

HOW READILY DOES YOUR CHILD ADAPT TO CHANGE?

Adaptability has to do with the ease with which a child can comfortably deal with changes — how easily they shift from one activity to another, and how well they flow with abrupt adjustments in plans and schedules. Because parents are often unaware of the adjustments they require their children to make, they may become annoyed when a child struggles.

Unexpected changes to schedules can throw some kids into a

tizzy. Just asking children to stop an activity and transition to something else may pose a challenge. Since all children need a measure of order and predictability, and few children function well without these, morning and evening rituals help children feel organized and safe.

"Turn off the television and come take your bath," may seem like a simple request, but to a slow-to-adapt child this can feel like a gigantic shift. If we take it to a larger level, experiences like moving to a new house, changes at school, going through a divorce, coping with a blended family, the arrival of a new baby, or even a visit from grandma can feel like too much to handle. Asking a slow-to-adapt child to deal with any type of change is like putting regular gasoline into a car that needs premium grade. If we expected the car to just "adapt" to the different grade, we would be in for a pretty bumpy ride.

When we ignore the reality of our child's wiring and expect a slow-to-adapt kid to adjust because we are the "boss," or because we are in a hurry, we trigger the very power struggles that drive us crazy. These children need consistent routines, with appropriate preparation when change is coming. Parents who set up transitions with advance notice of a shift, allow for choice, and encourage breathing time, help their slow-to-adjust child find a way to soothe themselves in a world that's constantly demanding instant adjustment.

We don't help children adjust to change by discounting their struggle. By acknowledging their need for help in adapting, we show them they have the ability to handle challenges. With patience and consistency, these kids begin to internalize the strategies we set up for them so they can handle the pressures that our fast-paced modern society demands.

If you have a household that's organized and predictable, and you are the kind of parent who needs time to adapt, you may find yourself thrown when you realize you are running late or your schedule has changed. When your child's behavior is the cause of an unexpected change of plan, you may overreact as a result of the anxiety you feel. In contrast, if you are flexible and comfortable with last-minute adaptations, you are likely to misunderstand a child who doesn't do well with hurrying or abrupt transitions.

Once again, you can't alter your child's natural wiring when it comes to adapting, whereas you can shift your thinking by telling yourself, "My child needs help in adapting to changes. This is true for daily transitions as well as for larger adjustments."

You may wish to use the following affirmations, which can help change your thinking:

I let go of the things I cannot control.

I cannot control my child's temperament — it's part of their unique cosmic design.

I accommodate to my child's ability to adapt and love them exactly as they are, allowing plenty of time to adjust to new situations.

I am a role model. I continue to nurture my own well-being and honor my own unique temperament.

My child and I are worthy of love, exactly as we are.

My intention is to extend the love that lives inside me to everything I think about my child and myself.

AUTHENTIC PARENTING POWER

You can help a child who is slow to adapt by saying, "You wish you didn't have to shut off the TV. I know it's hard for you. Your show will be over in a few minutes and it will be time to put on your pajamas."

When you understand that your child is resistant to new situations and transitions, you can prepare them. Help your child anticipate what's coming by talking about some of the things they can look forward to. Ask what would make the situation easier for them. A younger child might simply need to know you understand. Your willingness to be playful can also help ease morning and evening transitions.

"GET IN THERE AND MAKE ME PROUD"

CHILDREN HANDLE NEW SITUATIONS DIFFERENTLY

Initial reaction has to do with how your child handles new situations. Some children ease into unfamiliar surroundings, eagerly run over to a group of children, and are outgoing with family, teachers, and strangers. Other children withdraw from a new situation, cling to their parents' legs, or cry, rather than deal with the stress they feel.

There are times when resistant behavior embarrasses or disappoints us, especially when we want our children to behave in a way that makes us proud. We try to hide our own discomfort by saying "she's shy," not realizing that label feels to the child like a judgment. When we confuse children's legitimate discomfort with lack of respect or unwillingness to perform, we invalidate their unique hardwiring and impart the idea that something's wrong with them.

I have vivid memories of my son being outgoing and my daughter being tentative when approaching new situations. They even reacted differently when my mom came to visit. My son rushed into grandma's open arms, whereas my daughter either hid behind me or peeked out from her bedroom. Grandma was a gush of energy, and Melissa needed time to feel comfortable.

My mom interpreted Melissa's actions as rejection and became angry when she didn't shower her with kisses and hugs upon her arrival. I can still feel the hurt in my heart when I heard my mom tell my daughter she wouldn't play with her because she "didn't give grandma a hug." My mom didn't understand that Melissa's behavior originated from her hardwiring and had nothing to do with loving her grandma.

Some children are "energy readers." When they don't feel safe in a situation, they come across as slow to adapt. If you are cautious in new situations, especially when you don't feel comfortable, you can understand a child who needs time to warm up. If you move easily into new experiences, you may wonder why such situations are so stressful for your child. The trick is to handle the situation supportively by changing how you think about it. The following affirmations can help:

> I appreciate my child's caution and honor their need to move slowly into new situations.

> I trust that as they grow more comfortable with their ability to embrace new situations, they will find it easier to relax into them.

I am letting go of the things I can't control.

I can't control my child's temperament. It's part of their unique cosmic design.

I release my child's need to take time to adjust to new stimuli and love them exactly as they are, allowing plenty of time for them to feel comfortable with something new.

I am a role model for my child. I nurture my own well-being and honor my unique temperament.

My child and I are worthy of love, exactly as we are.

My intention is to extend the love that lives inside of me to everything I think about my child and myself.

You can help your cautious child by saying, "It's okay to take your time. You can watch first. I will stay close until you feel more comfortable." Then, give your child opportunities to practice getting comfortable with new situations. For instance, before kindergarten starts, arrange a visit to the classroom to see all the wonderful play areas. Before the soccer league begins, give them ample time to kick the ball around the yard. Sometimes, no matter what you do, this child will still need time to adjust. The best you can do is love them through it.

If your normally easy-to-adapt child suddenly shows signs of timidity or discomfort, it's possible they are picking up on uncomfortable energy. It's also possible something happened to cause them to feel less secure. A wise parent is willing to lovingly investigate.

"YOU'RE TOO SENSITIVE FOR YOUR OWN GOOD"

THINGS BOTHER SOME CHILDREN THAT DON'T BOTHER OTHERS

Physical sensitivity has to do with sensory hardwiring and affects the way a person responds to light, touch, noise, smells, movement, tags on clothing, temperature, the taste and texture of food, hunger, and fatigue. Some children seem to hardly notice these forms of stimulation, whereas others have built-in radar that's sensitive to just about everything in their environment.

A highly sensitive child can feel bombarded by their surroundings. The smells in a restaurant, noise in a room, number of people at a party, or volume of the television can all become irritants that spark strong reactions and turn a day of fun into an endurance test. It's as if these children experience life in 3D, while the rest of the family are having a two-dimensional experience. A day at the amusement park can end in a meltdown because of the long lines, crowds of people, smells, and other sensations. When not understood, these kids can seem really annoying and ungrateful.

Sensitive children are often judged by people who have never experienced sensation overload. Well-meaning adults send messages that something is wrong with these kids and they better grow a thick skin. However, instead of concluding that such children are spoiled, picky, fussy, or demanding, we can choose to imagine what it must feel like to live in their body. Once we appreciate the sensitivity of their perceptions, we are more willing to honor their reactions.

When my daughter was four years old, I bought her a party dress for a family gathering. It was purple with frills and lace. She jubilantly tried it on and agreed to wear it to the party. I had also bought matching socks and bows for her hair. The day of the party arrived, and we laughed and giggled as I got her ready. About thirty minutes later, as her brother, dad, and I were about to get into the car, she announced, "I don't want to wear this dress to the party." Beginning to pull the bows out of her carefully crafted ponytails, she added, "And take my hair down."

When she insisted on wearing an old dress that had been washed hundreds of times, I looked at my husband in disbelief, certain she was trying to sabotage my sanity.

It turned out that the new dress felt fine when she tried it on for five minutes, whereas after thirty minutes the new fabric was starting to itch, the ponytails were pulling and giving her a headache, and the new socks had seams that were bothering her toes. In contrast, the old dress was soft and comfortable.

Parents who attend my seminars always ask, "Did you make her wear the dress to the party?" The fact is, I can't remember. But I do remember feeling frustrated and angry. I didn't know then what I know now. Had I understood temperament, I would have washed the dress a few times, used fabric softener, and fixed her hair in a way that was more respectful of her sensitivity. Had none of this done the trick, I likely would have had to work on my ego and accept that she wouldn't walk into the party looking like my idea of the "perfect little girl."

Children who are born with extraordinary sensitivity are hypersensitive to the emotional and energetic climate in which they live. They can't be fooled with smiles or inauthentic reassurances. They can sense tension, fear, or judgment, and sometimes have difficulty regulating their reactions. Parents give a priceless gift to a sensitive child by honoring the delicate soul that needs to learn how to survive in this noisy, fast-paced, over-stimulating world.

If you are highly sensitive to smells, sounds, taste, fabrics, and the like, you can appreciate your child's overwhelmed reactions when bombarded by the environment. If you are on the low end of the sensitivity continuum, it may be hard to be patient with a child who gags on their food, has to leave a restaurant because the smells are overpowering, or slams their door because you refuse to lower the volume of the television.

In such a case, you can shift your thoughts by telling yourself, "My child's senses are highly attuned. They have the capacity to perceive things more subtly and keenly than most people. They are able to be empathic and deeply in touch with their emotions." Affirmations can prove helpful. I suggest the following:

I let go of the things I can't control.

My child's temperament is part of their unique cosmic design.

I love them exactly as they are.

I'm learning how to support sensitive children.

I am a role model to my child. I nurture my own well-being and honor my own unique temperament.

My child and I are worthy of love, exactly as we are.

My intention is to extend love and appreciation to both my child and myself.

You can help your sensitive child by saying, "I believe you when you say the eggs smell funny. How food tastes, smells, and looks is important to you. It smells and tastes good to me, but it doesn't smell good to you. You can choose something else."

Be mindful of your child's environment. Don't expect a sensitive child to be able to handle noisy, overcrowded, over-stimulating experiences without some quiet time. Be aware of how fabrics, fragrances, and other conditions might affect your sensitive child.

"AGAIN? WHAT'S WRONG WITH YOU?"

EVERY CHILD FEELS THINGS DIFFERENTLY

Strength of response has to do with how deeply children experience their emotions and how strongly they react. Intense children express their feelings in a big way, often confusing and frustrating their parents because they can be set off by what seems trivial to others. Low-intensity children express emotions with such slight changes of facial expression and tone of voice that parents often wonder what their child is feeling. Children at both ends of the intensity scale need understanding and support as they learn to express themselves in an effective manner.

A low-intensity child expresses both pleasure and discomfort in a subdued way, which means it's easy to miss what's going on inside these kids. We often label them as "good" because they seem to be less demanding, but it's important we don't ignore them and instead encourage their participation and expression of ideas.

The highly intense child lets everyone know how they feel in a really big way. These intense reactors may squeal with delight when happy and have meltdowns when frustrated. When young, they may hit, bite, throw toys, or have tantrums. Parents must be careful not to give them the message that they are "naughty," instead validating their feelings while setting firm limits for what's acceptable behavior. As these children grow older, adults often make the mistake of believing that if the child just tried harder, they could control their emotions, telling them to "get over themselves."

The intense two-year-old who wants a toy and is told "no" feels like their world is coming to an end. The seven-year-old who learns the picnic has been canceled rushes to their room sobbing with inconsolable disappointment. The ten-year-old who sees a movie about mistreated animals can't help crying whenever they think about cruelty. The teenager who was ridiculed on Facebook feels like killing themself. They are legitimately overwhelmed by their emotions, experiencing what *feels to them* like a "normal" reaction.

In an attempt to quell their reactivity, parents pass judgment, saying things such as:

- "Quit your acting."
- "I've had just about enough of this."
- "You're making a big deal out of nothing."
- "Just get over it already."

Being misunderstood amplifies the intense child's perception that something is wrong with them. To have their feelings overwhelm them *and* face retribution from their frustrated parents is a double whammy. Since they don't have the tools to soothe themselves, this can lead to a life of self-incrimination and anxiety.

Because intense parents approach life with passion and gusto, it's challenging when an intense parent and an intense child have strong reactions at the same time. The way forward is for the parent to work on their own strong reactions, since they don't always serve us well. A parent who rarely experiences big emotions may think their child is acting or being manipulative and make the mistake of demanding the child get their emotions under control. A wise parent's gift to an intense child is to appreciate the validity of their hardwiring, while patiently showing them how to soothe their overwhelming feelings and thereby regulate their reactions. Though you can't control your child's intensity, you can shift the way you think about it with the help of the following affirmations:

My child feels their feelings in a deep and passionate way.

I let go of things I can't control.

My child's temperament is part of their unique cosmic design.

I appreciate my child's intense temperament and love them exactly as they are.

I cherish their intensity and provide a safe space where they can experience their feelings. If they break down and have a tantrum, I don't take it as a personal attack. I realize that learning to soothe intense feelings takes time and practice.

I'm a role model. I nurture my own well-being. I express my feelings in a healthy way. I honor my unique temperament.

My child and I are worthy of love, exactly as we are.

My intention is to extend love and appreciation to both my child and myself.

Intense children are easily overcome by their emotions. When they break down into tearful fits they do not learn to soothe themselves by our judgments, time-outs or threats. They need us to understand how much they are struggling and at the same time they need us to stay calm and consistent in walking them through the process of expressing their feelings in appropriate ways.

We might say the following: " This is so hard for you. You wish it were different. I love you very much, even when you are upset and I will be here while you start to feel better." If the child hits, spits, kicks or demands that we do something, we calmly respond, "You are feeling big feelings. I hear you. It is OK to cry. I won't let you hurt anyone" or "I will help you remember the rules." We can move away from the child or remove them from a situation with loving energy and at the same time stick to our standards.

Whether we are home or out in public, our intention is not to punish but to help the child learn how to self-soothe overwhelming emotions. As the hysterics start to subside we can encourage them to take deep breaths. (It is helpful for us to breathe as well because in order to be effective we must stay connected to our own inner calm.)

The goal is to reconnect the child to their natural state of well-being. Once they begin to feel better we can keep the good energy flowing by reminding them of positive choices that are in that moment available to them. There is no need for punishment. Both parent and child are learning that this was just a blip in the day and there is no need to continue the suffering.

We can establish clear boundaries in advance by reminding our intense child that we will not change our mind just because they have strong emotions. Before leaving the house make it clear (in a loving manner) that big reactions will signal that it is time to find a quiet place to calm down and regroup before returning to a public place. At times, we may just have to return home, reminding our child (and our tired, cranky self) that there will always be a chance to try again.

Our willingness to perceive this behavior as a legitimate struggle and our patient, non-punitive, ever appreciating progress will prove to establish a trusting bond that will last for a lifetime.

As the intense child matures, they will continue to learn how to soothe the inner stress created by a flood of emotions without the added burden of self-judgment, unworthiness or the need to escape into alcohol or drugs. It is a life-long learning experience for intense people to realize that the way in which they deliver a message is as important as the content of the message.

"STOP DAYDREAMING AND FOCUS"

HOW EASILY IS YOUR CHILD DISTRACTED?

Distractibility has to do with a child's ability to concentrate on a task uninterrupted by either external stimuli or their own thoughts. Some children have good intentions but are easily distracted. Morning routines can be sidetracked by something as innocent as seeing a toy lying on the floor. While some children can walk right by the toy, able to focus on getting washed and dressed, an easily distracted child may forget the task at hand and get lost in play. It's crucial not to judge such behavior as good or bad. The easily distracted child isn't "naughty" or "irresponsible." Yelling at them to focus won't change their hardwiring.

It's particularly common for toddlers to be distracted. Used as a technique for changing a toddler's focus, distraction can actually be an effective way to divert a small child from getting into mischief. A two-year-old moving toward an electric cord can easily have their attention refocused by a squeaky toy. However, distraction becomes a concern when an older child tends to get sidetracked or lost in daydreaming when they are supposed to be focusing on a task.

With ADHD now prevalent, it can be helpful to have a professional determine whether a child has high distractibility or a neurological condition related to ADHD. There's also considerable debate about whether the indicators for ADHD are simply normal behavior at the extreme of the distractibility scale. My sense is that we need to be slow to label and medicate.

Children who are easily distracted need help staying focused. While it can be frustrating to live with these kids, parents who chastise their children cause increased inner turmoil for a child who is already struggling to keep up with daily demands.

As a parent, if you are highly distractible, you may find yourself worrying about your highly distractible child because you don't want them to suffer the consequences you experienced in school or out in the world. If you are at the low end of distractibility, you may mistakenly think your child could focus more if only they tried harder.

Even though you can't control your child's ability to stay focused, you can change the way you think about it. The following affirmations may be helpful:

My child notices everything that's going on around them. They are bright, creative, and think outside the box.

My child's temperament is part of their unique cosmic design.

I allow plenty of time for my child to get their tasks done, and I create sufficient organization and structure.

I'm a role model for my child. I nurture my own well-being and honor my unique temperament.

My child and I are worthy of love, exactly as we are.

My intention is to extend the love that lives inside me to everything I think about both my child and myself.

You can help your easily distracted child by saying, "Let's find a way that will help you." Be present and walk your child through routines instead of leaving them on their own. Keep tasks short with timely check-ins. Create an environment free of distraction, such as noise from television or accessibility to a computer.

"HOW MANY TIMES DO I HAVE TO TELL YOU THE ANSWER IS 'NO'?"

THE CHILD WHO JUST NEVER GIVES UP

Highly persistent children have a hard time shifting their focus. They struggle when interrupted during a task, which means they need time to finish things that are important to them. When they are unsure of how their needs are going to be met, they inevitably experience inner turmoil.

For instance, your four-year-old is building with Legos. When you call them to dinner, they ignore you. You shout again, "Put those blocks down, wash your hands, and come to the table." If they continue to play, it's likely you have a highly persistent child, which means it's challenging for them to tear themselves away from their activity.

Children like this are often labeled as stubborn, strong-willed, or difficult. You may be tempted either to scold them for being disobedient or give in to avoid confrontation.

Very persistent children also have a hard time accepting "no" for an answer. They argue their point, asking the same questions over and over, insisting they get what they want. This isn't because they are trying to give you a hard time, but because they can't tolerate the inner urgency they experience. In an honest attempt to feel validated, they may become manipulative.

You can teach these kids how to manage their sense of internal tension by setting up their day so they can make choices within a framework of consistent rules and limits.

For example, a seven-year-old can know that the soda limit is one glass per day and be allowed to choose when to drink it. At first they'll likely drink it so early that they'll beg for more. With consistent reinforcement, you can help them plan the timing of their sweets. An older child needs a consistent, predictable routine of completing their homework and chores before they begin playing a video game. In this way they will be less inclined to attempt to negotiate a deal that gets them out of meeting their responsibilities.

At the other extreme are children with low persistence who are easily frustrated and tend to get upset as soon as something doesn't go their way. They may give up on a demanding task or have a hard time waiting for help. For instance, your eight-year-old may be struggling with their math homework. After doing three exercises, they shut the book and say they are done. Children like this often become labeled as lazy or manipulative. You know they could do better if they only tried harder. The older the child is, the trickier it is to know for sure whether this is pure temperament or influenced by boredom, low self-esteem, or just not enjoying the task at hand. You can support this child by resisting your urge to tease or intimidate them into completing tasks and instead, offer natural rewards and expressions of appreciation for sticking with a challenge. Natural rewards include hugs, high fives, time spent together on a fun activity, points toward a coveted toy or the privilege to join a team. Parents must also be careful not to take over the child's schoolwork as a way of soothing their own fears about the future. It takes courage to allow our children to experience the natural consequences of their actions and it takes wisdom to discern if the school environment is conducive to this particular child's learning style.

If you are highly persistent, it may drive you crazy when you are interrupted by your children's demands for attention. Some highly persistent adults have such high standards of accomplishment for themselves, they have little time or energy left to nurture their children. Their long to-do list can get in the way of feeling pleasure or having fun. You can't control your child's level of persistence, but you can change the way you think about it with the following affirmations:

My highly persistent child is hardwired to keep trying and doesn't give up until they accomplish their goal. Someday this will serve them well.

My easily frustrated child is hardwired to want to give up when things are challenging. As they grow older, they will discover their ability to pursue their goals and complete tasks.

I can't control what's important to my child. I release the need to convince my child that what's important to me should be important to them.

RECOGNIZE AND RESPOND TO YOUR CHILD'S SPECIFIC TEMPERAMENT

I can't control my child's temperament. It's part of their unique cosmic design.

I'm a role model to my child as I nurture my own well-being and honor my unique temperament.

My child and I are worthy of love, exactly as we are.

My intention is to extend the love that lives inside me to everything I think about both my child and myself.

You can help your highly persistent child by saying, "It's important to you to finish, and we'll save it so you can finish it later. We have to go now." Or you might say, "You would really like me to agree to let you go with your friends to see the movie. I hear that it's important to you and wish I felt comfortable letting you go. I'm not going to change my mind because I think the movie is inappropriate. Let's talk about other movie choices that I'm comfortable with you seeing." Keep your word. If you tell your child they can finish something later or you are open to alternatives, make sure you earn their trust by following through.

HAVE YOU COME TO TERMS WITH YOUR
OWN UNIQUE TEMPERAMENT?

Like children, parents have their own unique physical blueprints. Once you acknowledge your own temperament and style of being, you take a big step toward understanding the way cosmic design influences our perception of our experiences. While some parents relate easily to a child whose temperament is similar to their own, others find they are in a constant battle. Some of us don't realize that our own temperament is causing many of the power struggles. Even with the best of intentions, it's never wise to try to manipulate another person's hardwiring, since it leads to frustration for everyone. As parents, our power lies in understanding the way each person interprets the world. No one is wrong. Each one of us is having a valid experience. Conflict arises when we expect everyone to hear the same beat to different drums.

The aim is to thrive within our temperamental blueprint, learning how to soothe ourselves and fulfill our life's purpose as we work through the challenges of our unique design. The human spirit is wounded when a parent doesn't understand their own, their mate's, or their children's individual temperaments.

Though hardwiring is never an excuse for inappropriate behavior by either an adult or a child, when we don't understand the power of hardwiring, we can misunderstand what's happening and create an emotional mess. For example, Sarah asked her four-year-old daughter if she would like to go to their local pasta restaurant for dinner. Moriah's intense wiring was instantly activated. "Oh, yes," she enthused, hardly able to contain her excitement as she ran into her father's office to tell him to hurry up and get ready. Because Moriah didn't know how to soothe herself during the thirty minutes until it was time to leave, her father — also an intense reactor — became annoyed, as he was in the middle of composing an important email. Unless Moriah could play quietly for the next half hour, he threatened to cancel their dinner plans.

Sarah, sensitive to both her child's and her husband's intensity, moved in to placate everyone, suggesting she help Moriah get ready. She had put out a freshly washed outfit, but Moriah didn't want to wear it, instead insisting on wearing her princess shirt, which had just been put in the dirty laundry. Mom, being naturally persistent and not wanting to give into her daughter's demands, explained that Moriah couldn't wear a soiled shirt. Equally persistent, Moriah insisted she just had to wear that shirt. Dad, being sensitive to noise, found he couldn't concentrate because of the bickering and burst into the bedroom, demanding they tone down the arguing. When Moriah started to cry, mom threw up her hands, declaring that both her daughter and husband were impossible.

With the joy of going out to dinner lost in the emotional storm, mom and dad both agreed that if only Moriah had acted differently, they all would have experienced a nice time together. They ignored their own behavior and insisted that only 'good girls' who listen to their parents deserve to go out to eat. Moriah was left believing that the disastrous evening was all her fault. Feeling the confusion caused by shame and loneliness, Moriah went to bed sobbing.

No one felt good that night. Both parents felt overwhelmed, unappreciated and frustrated.

While basic temperament was a powerful factor in the way each family member reacted to the events of the evening, it was the judgment and blaming that actually caused the negative turn of events.

Once parents realize that the contrasts of differing temperaments are not an indication that something is wrong and may actually be gifts that promote growth, they can stop allowing the challenges to become triggers of blame or rage. Your work is not to change anyone else but to learn how to soothe yourself so your sense of well-being becomes the dominant force in your reactions.

Moriah's parents can learn to do this. The night could have turned out differently. You can do it too. It takes willingness and practice. You do not have to do it perfectly. The important thing to remember is that no temperamental trait means that a person is flawed. You can stop judging and blaming each other for the ways you are triggered. At the heart of authentic parenting is a grown up who is ready to make peace with each family member's hard wiring and use that as a platform for growing both emotionally and spiritually.

CHAPTER 3

AGES AND STAGES

"Don't worry that children never listen to you;
worry that they are always watching you."

— Robert Fulghum

DEVELOPMENTAL STAGES

"Ages and stages" is a professional expression that describes a predictable sequence of behaviors that are to be expected as children progress through the first eighteen years of life. While parents have no control over each child's cosmic blueprint, they can influence the manner in which the home environment either nourishes or hinders healthy development as each of these stages presents itself.

At the heart of most struggles is a parent who misunderstands the cause of their child's actions. Many so-called "problem" behaviors are normal and, at certain ages, to be expected. We become empowered by learning what's typical, so we can anticipate and respond with age-appropriate, emotionally healthy strategies. It's time to move away from the old notion that punishing a child teaches them a lesson. The only lesson it teaches is to mistrust us.

Equally unhealthy is the parent who is uncomfortable setting appropriate limits. Children learn compassion, responsibility, and self-control through repeated opportunities to rework impulses. Parents who indulge poor behavior don't help their kids tolerate frustration or develop the self-discipline it takes to make good choices. Children raised by permissive parents don't grow up feeling like the parent is a friend. On the contrary, when children can't trust their parents to enforce standards, they learn to disrespect the parent and eventually become more challenging.

Children thrive with age-appropriate limits that are consistently upheld in an environment of empathy and compassion. They don't work out solutions in a timeout chair. Neither do they work out solutions when they are rescued from challenges.

A balanced approach begins with understanding the emotions and behaviors that are to be expected, coupled with a knowledge of the most effective ways to handle them. Parents become empowered when they shift their focus from demanding immediate compliance to building relationships of empathy and trust.

Within each developmental stage lie the seeds for nurturing a transformative relationship between parent and child. Self-worth and a sense of wholeness flourish when parents are willing to see the world through the ever-changing perceptions of their infant, toddler, school-aged child, or teen.

Each stage of development presents challenges that require parents to be aware, so they don't take behavior personally or react in the heat of the moment. There are bound to be numerous challenging behaviors, depending on your child's temperament, perceptions, and family circumstances. A crucial component of a child's sense of self is how we handle each situation. Our voice is internalized as our children receive messages either of understanding and affirmation, or of judgment and condemnation. The way we set up the environment and our style of responding to daily interactions lets them know whether it's safe to make mistakes, whether we trust their ability to make good decisions, and whether life holds the promise of a joyful adventure or shame and punishment.

While the following behaviors that typically trouble parents are often quite normal, it's important to note that these behaviors in excess may signal a need for professional help:

- It's normal for a child to feel jealous and regress after the birth of a new sibling.

- It's normal for a young child to want to sleep in their parents' bed to feel safe.

- It's normal for a child to have nightmares after seeing scary movies or listening to the evening news.

- It's normal for children to start doing poorly in school after the divorce of their parents.

- It's normal for children to lie when they don't feel safe telling the truth.

- It's normal for children to manipulate if they don't trust that their needs will be met.

- It's normal for children to whine if they don't believe they will be heard.

- It's normal for children to be messy, make mistakes, push the rules, forget about limits, and ask lots of questions.

- It's normal for young children to seek lots of attention and for teenagers to seek autonomy while demanding privacy.

- It's normal for children to want to make their own decisions and have their viewpoint respected.

- It's normal for teenagers to be moody and to want to spend time alone.

As one stage of a child's development morphs into the next, a parent stays empowered by learning what to expect and remembering what it must feel like to be going through that stage of development.

WHAT TO EXPECT AT DIFFERENT AGES

It's important to remember that not every child experiences challenges in the same way or on the same timeline, which means we should never compare children. Our overall message must be, "I see you. I hear you. Your challenging behavior doesn't make you naughty. We'll figure it out together so we both feel better. You are loved and worthy exactly as you are."

It can be helpful to know what a child would say at each stage of their development if they could speak their truth:

The Infant Stage *(birth-1)* I'm sensitive to your moods and am tuned into your energy. I'm adjusting to life on earth and learning to trust that this is a safe place. Don't be fooled by how tiny I am. There's a wise soul within my little body.

I need to bond with one consistent adult who knows how to read my signals and doesn't feel anxious when I cry. I need you to manage your own stress so that when you are with me, I feel soothed and secure. Please don't make decisions about my well-being from a place of fear.

You can help me by taking good care of your own needs and being relaxed when you are with me. Validate my anxiety around strangers and don't expect me to be okay with being handed off to other adults.

Please don't define me as "good" when I lie still and "bad" when I cry. My crying is a form of communication. I am infinite potential, figuring out how to be okay in a human body. I'm here to become my own person.

I've come to enrich your life. Cherish our quiet moments together. Once I start walking, I'll turn your world upside down.

Please give me these messages: "I'm so happy you are here. We're going to have so much fun together. This is the place where you belong. I'll take good care of you. I love holding you, breathing with you, and just being with you. I'll be patient with you."

The Toddler Stage *(1-3)* I'm an energized, self-centered explorer, needing constant supervision. I insist on doing things by myself, leaving a messy trail wherever I go. My favorite words "no" and "mine" express how I experience the world. I have no sense of time and live in the present moment. I'm resistant to change, impulsive, easily distracted, finicky, and can quickly resort to a tantrum when I'm tired, hungry, over-stimulated, or expected to do something I can't easily do. Transitions are difficult, and sharing is nearly impossible for me. I sometimes express my emotions by hitting or biting because I haven't yet figured out what else to do. I learn best by watching you, copying your language and actions. I don't mean to exhaust you or make you angry. I'm just not able to do many of the things you wish I could do.

I need you to put me in environments that are safe for exploration because I will touch, taste, run, and climb on everything in reach. I need you to anticipate my meltdowns and not expect me to share, sit still, remember limits, or understand intellectual explanations. I need lots of positive attention and will be most cooperative when you give me choices, using fun and humor to distract me. If you laugh when I do the wrong thing, I'll think you want me to repeat it.

You can help me find my voice by putting language to what I'm experiencing. Smile and hug me when I get things right. Patiently redirect me when I forget the limits. Predictable routines and consistent expectations help me cooperate with you. If I mess up, please don't take my behavior personally, because I struggle between declaring independence and needing you desperately. I beg you not to compare me with your friends' kids; rather, just encourage me to discover who I am.

I've come to rock your world. Slow down and enjoy our hectic and often chaotic toddler roller coaster ride. These two years are laying the groundwork of our relationship, and I want more than anything to feel secure in your joyful, unconditional love. Think of these years as exciting rather than terrible, because my brain is at its height of development and I'm learning so much.

Please give me these messages: "We feel joyful as we watch you think for yourself, exploring and discovering how things work. We know you'll test limits and won't always listen to us. It's okay to feel your power, to say "no," and to want to do things yourself. We will guide you in finding the balance between your desire to be independent and your need for closeness and security."

Pre-School *(3-5)* I can be talkative, assertive, bossy, boastful, argumentative, explosive, destructive, and impatient. I sometimes grab, hit, test limits, exaggerate, and tease. I'm meant to be an adventurer with a vivid imagination, which means I struggle with taking turns, being patient, standing in line, or sitting still.

I need you to give me choices, appreciate my opinions, validate my imagination, acknowledge my concerns and fears, and allow me plenty of time to play and move my whole body. I may be little, but I have some really great ideas and it's important you value them.

You can help me by understanding that even if I'm the big brother or sister, I still need special time with you. I do best with a predictable routine and consistent, compassionate, firm reinforcement. Telling me what I *can* do and using encouragement to reinforce what I've done well helps me repeat desirable behavior. When I sense you understand me, I think you are my best friend in the whole wide world. But when it feels like you don't understand me, I may tell you I hate you.

I'm figuring out who I am. Please don't make clean rooms and eating vegetables more important than our relationship. Help me be responsible without yelling at me or making me feel bad about myself. Keep your standards high and be sure to notice when I do something well.

Please give me these messages: "We love you exactly as you are. You don't have to change for us to feel good. You are capable, intelligent, powerful, and important. You can trust us to listen to you without judgment and to give you compassionate and honest feedback. You can grow up to be anything you truly want to be that fits your blueprint."

School Age *(6-10)* I'm moving out into the world, becoming self-confident and independent. I'm learning to navigate the pressures of school and my own emotions. Friendships are important, though I sometimes struggle with seeing other people's point of view. I can be a know-it-all and critical of others. Sometimes

I'm too judgmental of myself.

I need predictable routines, family rituals, and consistent limits that make sense and seem fair. These help me feel safe as I explore the world. If I'm too opinionated or seem moody, please understand that I'm sometimes overwhelmed by my emotions.

You can help me by being a positive role model. I watch the way you operate in the world, how you treat people, handle your own emotions, and deal with challenges. Please spend special time with me, where our only goal is to build our relationship. Notice my efforts and take time to appreciate my positive attributes. Don't be quick to point out my faults. Help me solve problems by asking me open-ended questions that encourage me to think about how my behavior affects others and whether it gets me the results I want.

I may remind you of yourself when you were my age. Don't expect me to be a copy of you, and don't worry that I will become your fears. Allow me to dream my own dreams, and trust that my journey will unfold exactly as it needs to.

Please give me these messages: "You are figuring out who you are. You can feel powerful and capable, yet still ask for our advice when you need it. All of your feelings are okay with us. Even when we disagree, we still love and adore you. Mistakes are opportunities to learn and to grow."

Tweens *(11-13)* I'm going through huge physiological changes. My growing sense of independence and heightened emotional sensitivity may cause us to misunderstand each other. I'm dealing with the overwhelming challenges of middle school, peer pressure, my changing body, and the influence of social media. I have a strong pull to my friends. I sometimes question and challenge authority. If I'm angry or defiant, it may be a signal I need more of your love, attention, and help.

I need you not to take my behavior personally. Speaking to me in a calm and respectful voice, even when you are upset with me, will make it easier for me to treat you with respect. I need to believe you understand how I'm struggling and that I desperately need to feel like I'm loved and understood in my own home.

You can help me by having clear and consistent standards and expectations. If you don't model these standards in your own behavior, I'll judge you to be a hypocrite and become rebellious. It's really helpful if you can be flexible as we negotiate expectations together. It will also help if you educate me about the possible consequences of my actions.

There will be times when I hold up an energetic mirror and force our family to take off our masks of propriety and see ourselves as we really are. This crucial time in my development is an opportunity for us all to reevaluate our beliefs and way of being.

Please give me these messages: "You are figuring out who you are and how you fit into the world. You can trust your feelings to guide you. It's okay to disagree with us and even to argue with us. This will help us all clarify what we believe. Your ideas are valuable. You are worthy and capable, regardless of your mistakes."

Teens *(14-18)* I'm going through a period of crisis as I come to terms with my identity. I struggle with feeling awkward, anxious, insecure, self-doubting, overwhelmed, and at times out of control. My behavior is confusing, as I can be contrary, disobedient, rebellious, restless, and intensely private. I want to be accepted by my peers and I'm self-conscious about my body. In my craving for independence, I may behave in inconsistent and unpredictable ways.

I need you to understand the enormous struggle I'm experiencing as I navigate life's conflicting messages and overwhelming responsibilities. Be sympathetic, but please resist the desire to always intervene. Allow me to make my own choices and to experience the effects of my decisions. Never lament that my future is doomed or that I'm a disappointment to the family. I truly want to be a compassionate, empathic person, but peer, school, and family pressures often cause me to disconnect from my best self.

You can help me by being an authentic role model. When I watch you express gratitude and forgiveness, I'm reminded that seeing the good in others and displaying acts of kindness is possible. When you speak to me from a heart-centered place, I'm able to connect with my own intuition. Please don't lecture me or try to control me through guilt, shame, or fear, for I'll shut down to you and seek love and acceptance in all the wrong places. Remember that this is just a phase of my development, so hold the vision of me as a well-adjusted, happy adult.

I came to experience my own unique journey and to express my personal vision in this ever-expanding world. My path may be different from the one you might have chosen for me. Know that I ache to repair the hurts of my growing years and ask you to keep your heart soft and open as I become an adult and walk alongside you.

Please give me these messages: "You are learning many important lessons about life, friendships, work, and relationships. We enjoy watching you develop into your own unique person with fresh ideas and interests, even when these are different from ours. You are maturing by taking responsibility for your beliefs, behavior, needs, and feelings. As you branch out into the world, you can always come to us for guidance and support."

CHANGE YOUR "WAR STORIES"

Part of the human paradox is that we all desire happiness, yet we focus much of our attention on the things that upset us. When we listen to ourselves and our friends as we share stories about our children's challenging behavior, it's almost as if we try to top each other with tales of frustration and defiance. However, blaming and complaining usually leave us feeling ineffective and powerless.

Our power lies in the way we choose to tell our story. If we knew for sure our children would grow into thriving adults without insisting they comply with our expectations, would we be more willing to keep our focus on building a healthy emotional relationship with them?

Instead of lamenting their irresponsibility, messiness, orneriness, lack of focus, and propensity to fight with siblings, we can tell the story of their attributes, progress, and successes. Believe yourself when you explain to disapproving family and friends that typical behavior isn't manipulation or disrespect, and that developmental struggles are legitimate, whether we are the parent or the child.

The challenges of each stage are compounded by the way the issues of the previous stages were handled. If threats, punishments, shame, or angry timeouts were the dominant form of adult response, the next development stage will be affected by delayed growth. The natural swings from states of equilibrium to periods of meltdown, from sweet cooperation to outright rebellion, are all part of being human. No parent can escape the inevitable stages of child development. Just when you think you have a stage figured out, the kids are on to the next one.

When children move through the contrasts that each stage brings, it becomes tricky for adults to figure out if specific behavior is propelled by the pre-disposition of temperament, a legitimate need, typical development, or environmental factors. My experience has convinced me that it is usually a combination of all of these. Your ability to welcome situations exactly as they are, combined with a willingness to give up judgment and blame, open up the ability to wonder about the child's inner world. Each challenge becomes an opportunity to readjust expectations and responses. It also is a vehicle for establishing channels of communication and developing trust.

Along the way you must re-evaluate the meaning of discipline as you seek an authentic approach to encouraging emotionally healthy habits of excellence.

CHAPTER 4

CREATE HABITS OF EXCELLENCE

"We are what we repeatedly do.
Excellence therefore, is not an act but a habit."

— Aristotle

DELIBERATE PARENTING

Understanding typical developmental challenges never means the home becomes a free-for-all. It does mean we are purposeful as we create an environment that's physically and emotionally set up for success. The key to this is our self-discipline as parents, so that we model clear standards of behavior. Modeling is far more effective than preaching what we don't live.

Moving into the experience of becoming a parent is an adult stage of development. As we do so, it's important that our behavior is that of a truly mature adult. This requires us to be mindful of the habits of thinking, reacting, and responding we've created for ourselves.

In the business and education worlds, the expression "best practices" is used to describe techniques that consistently show results superior to those achieved via other methods. Parents who are willing to create a vision for their family, and patiently give their time and energy to stretch themselves past old-fashioned discipline paradigms, experience the miracle of authentic cooperation that results from such best practices.

If you have a parenting partner, it's important to work with them to articulate the values you want to model for your children —

to agree as a couple on what constitute best practices. Most of us become parents without giving much thought to the emotional environment we will create for our children and what guiding principles will direct our decisions. For this reason I recommend parents sit down together and talk about their approach to parenting.

Children learn what they see lived by their parents, together with what they experience for themselves, not what's preached at them. It's therefore essential to decide the kind of parents we want to be. What qualities do we want to exhibit for our children? Using our own core values as a framework for reflection, we can challenge ourselves to be an example of respect, kindness, and responsibility in all of our dealings with our family members.

I often hear parents say to their kids, "Get over here right now or you'll get a spanking." Another threat is, "I'll give you to the count of three, then I'll take away your iPad." Still another is, "If you don't listen to me, you'll go in the timeout chair as soon as we get home." None of these are either kind or respectful. When we fail to demonstrate best practices in the way we relate in such everyday matters, how can we expect our children to be kind and respectful?

On the other hand, I hear parents say things like, "It looks like you're having a hard time putting away your toys. Would you like some help?" Or they may say, "You're angry that your sister went into your room without asking permission. You can tell her how angry you feel." I also hear parents say, "I appreciate your bringing the dishes to the sink. It's really helpful." Such statements model understanding, kindness, and respect, which teach children to behave in the same ways they see us behave.

It isn't only in direct communication with our children that it's crucial we speak respectfully. When we think about or talk about a child, it's important not to make jokes or judgmental statements about them. Demeaning expressions such as the "terrible twos," "brat," "manipulator," "lazy," and "monster" should be replaced with descriptions that honor the child's experience. If we speak this way, the attitude such words convey will inevitably spill over into how we relate to a child.

Instead, we can discuss a child by saying things like, "They are exploring, discovering, and expressing their need to feel independent." We can then wonder whether our environment is one that effectively meets their stage of development. Or we might say, "While math is challenging, they have a brilliant and inquisitive mind." We can wonder whether we engage them in conversations and experiences that use math concepts in a fun way. By reflecting in this manner, we soothe ourselves and are more affective when facing daily challenges.

TIME TO REEVALUATE DISCIPLINE

Parents fool themselves when they believe it's okay to treat their children with angry, disrespectful, threatening discipline techniques, all the while proclaiming they are doing these things because they "love" the child. Spanking, hitting, screaming, threatening, and the use of sarcasm are an indication the parent hasn't yet discovered their true parenting power. We should never blame a child for our own unacceptable behavior nor should we fool ourselves that such techniques are beneficial in nurturing physically or emotionally healthy adults.

The goal of parenting is for a child to become self-disciplined, so that they bring forth their own internal wisdom. Society creates fear in a parent, taking away their natural trust that a child will grow into their own wisdom. If a parent reacts from their own fear, they won't parent in an emotionally healthy way.

Many adults see discipline as adhering to external standards, such as cultivating an exercise routine, sticking to a diet and having a long career in a job they might actually hate. I see self-discipline as being deliberate in staying connected to a state of physical, emotional and spiritual well-being. It is from this place that we can live a balanced life based on respect, integrity, responsibility, compassion and joy.

Cultivating self-discipline in a child begins with the parent becoming self-disciplined. Each of us is our child's most influential teacher, so it's our responsibility to discipline ourselves as we learn strategies that not only serve our children's well-being in the moment but also lay the foundation for healthy emotional development.

A misunderstanding of discipline eats away at the fabric of a healthy relationship between parents and children. Fear of raising an irresponsible child can drive a parent to have a meltdown at the sight of an unmade bed. Fear of disease can lead a parent to create power struggles over eating healthy food and engaging in proper daily hygiene. Fear of not getting into a prestigious university can drive a parent to shame a child who is legitimately struggling in school.

To teach effectively requires being mindful in our lives in a manner that invites success. Becoming organized ourselves, learning nonviolent communication techniques, setting up consistent expectations and routines, responding in a predictable manner, and engaging older children in conversations that create standards of mutual respect, are all part of teaching a child self-discipline. While there may be times when children have to listen simply because we are the parent, such as in matters of safety, this can't be our primary mode of moving through a day.

CREATE GUIDELINES THAT FOSTER WELL-BEING

When a limit is perceived as illogical, imposed simply because a parent has authority, it's natural for a child to feel rebellious. When a limit makes sense and helps a child feel safe, the child is more apt to conform to it. When parents make rules that are inconsistently enforced or not modeled by the parents themselves, most children tend to resist.

While some children are outwardly contemptuous of such discipline, others shrink into a state of inner turmoil, doing as they are told, but secretly living with confusion and fear. These kids may eventually exhibit physical ailments or emotional issues. Concerned parents often take them to physicians and psychologists, hoping for a diagnosis that can be fixed with medication. Unfortunately, even the medical community often misses the underlying symptoms that stem from the illusions created by unhealthy discipline strategies or well meaning parents who do not know how to make emotional connections. These kids are put on medications that merely control the symptoms and dull their sparkle.

Dr. Bernie Siegel's groundbreaking book, "Love, Medicine and Miracles" makes the compelling argument that scientific research insists that, "Unconditional love is the most powerful stimulant of the immune system. The truth is: love heals."

Unconditionally loving limits teach children how to live in their highest integrity, not simply to acquiesce to authority. Sensible limits are based on natural and logical consequences. For instance, limiting the intake of sweets isn't about controlling behavior; rather, it's to teach your child how to love their body.

Children who generally feel empowered tend to flow with reasonable limits, while those who often feel disempowered get their dignity back by resisting.

The empowered parent looks at conflicts as what, when I trained educators, we referred to as "teachable moments." Such moments require the adult to be attuned to what's important to the child, which enables us to turn that moment into a bonding experience, encouraging trust, closeness, curiosity, and creativity.

LEARN TO IDENTIFY TEACHABLE MOMENTS

The discipline in a teachable moment always has at its basis, a conscious desire to preserve the dignity and unlock the potential of each person involved. When we look at situations as teachable moments, we shift from interpreting disputes as indications of disrespect. Instead, we perceive the encounter as an honest quest for getting needs met. Within this framework, the adult becomes a powerful teacher and sets the stage with compassionate communication. When parents and children are encouraged to express their truth, safe from judgment, these moments morph into relationships based on mutual respect, empathy, and authentic cooperation.

In this teachable moment scenario, a four-year-old boy is

building with blocks in the family room, located off the kitchen. The mother is preparing dinner. The two-year-old sibling wakes up from a late afternoon nap and toddles over to the construction site. As he plops downs, eager to join in the fun, the older child screams, "Get away from here." The little one picks up a block and flings it across the room. The mother has to stop her work and intervene before someone gets hurt.

This is the moment when a fairy godmother's presence would be greatly appreciated, but the only adult available is an exhausted mom. The typical reaction from a parent doesn't take into account the older brother's inability to put his own needs on hold in order to make life easier for his mom or his younger sibling. The mother's reaction is to suggest that the four-year-old let the toddler play with him. "You should share with your brother," she says. "He just wants to be with you."

"No, Mom, he wrecks everything," argues the older boy. "He's going to break my building." How does he know this? It is likely that he is remembering past experiences.

The tired mother simply wants the boys to be peaceful so she can get dinner on the table. "Give him some blocks and let him build with you," she suggests.

"I don't want him here," shrieks the older child, refusing to take on the responsibility of his younger brother. "Take him away."

"I hear you," the mother says, "but these blocks belong to your brother too, so you need to share."

Observe how the mother is not only ignoring past experiences, but also isn't hearing what her older child is saying because she's operating in "wishing mode" instead of in reality. Though some four-year-olds are capable of happily handing over a bunch of blocks, a more-typical reaction is for the older sibling to become angry, knock down his building, then pout.

In these kinds of situations adults often don't know what to do. They just want the older brother to put his own needs on hold. This would certainly make everyone's life easier, but at the cost of invalidating the older child's truth. When we ignore a child's perspective, we create the very power struggles we hate because we are teaching the child to shut down their feelings in order to please others. This carries the ramification of also teaching them we aren't to be trusted to act in their best interests.

How would an empowered parent handle this? Setting up an environment for success doesn't mean conflicts won't arise. However, an empowered parent anticipates typical challenges and is prepared for the teachable moment, even though it never seems to come at a convenient time. Changing our thinking from "Who needs this right now?" to "This is a teachable moment" is a key aspect of parental power.

HOW TO HANDLE THE CHALLENGE OF SIBLINGS

There are several ways a parent can prepare for such an inevitable sibling challenge:

Think general thoughts:

- It's difficult for siblings to share. It's part of the learning process. Neither of them is being naughty. It's a legitimate struggle for both of them.

- There are no magical answers. I'm not a bad parent because I sometimes lose patience. I can figure this out.

Prepare in advance. You can borrow strategies from the best preschool teachers:

- Give each child a box of blocks and Legos labeled with their photograph and name. (This is a great idea for all toys and an excellent pre-reading tool.)

- Establish a consistent expectation: Children will use their own blocks and may not take from each other without permission. (This teaches respect for each other's property.)

- Spend lots of time patiently playing with the children, modeling the skills of asking permission, waiting turns and soothing disappointment.

- Understand that transitions are challenging for young children and be prepared to suspend dinner preparations to help both children adjust.

- Realize that even with the best-planned strategies, toddlers are unpredictable. Remind the older child in advance that once the toddler awakens, he will have the additional choice of moving his project to a separate room or joining in another activity. Since you will be busy preparing dinner, you won't be able to sit with them for a long time.

- Have an alternative activity ready. For instance, prepare fresh play dough for the children to use while you finish preparing dinner.

If the children begin to argue, see it as an opportunity to model effective communication skills:

- Observe what's happening and make a nonjudgmental statement such as, "I see your brother is interrupting you building your castle. You wish he would play with his own blocks and leave you alone."

- Talk about your feelings. Inquire into their feelings. You might say, "You are so angry that David is touching your cars. I feel sad that I can't help you share right now."

- Talk about your needs and inquire into their needs by saying, "I need to get dinner ready. I don't want to hear you fighting about the blocks. I wonder whether you need me to help you find something else to do."

- Talk about actions that are possible options such as, "I can help you move your blocks to your room, where you can continue to build by yourself." Or, "I made some soft, squishy play dough. You can sit at the counter and play with the play dough while I finish getting dinner ready." In such a context, your energy, playfulness, and joyfulness can prove contagious.

By anticipating recurring issues, we avoid feeling annoyed when they pop up. By talking about the challenge in a nonjudgmental way, we create a safe moment of learning. We recognize feelings and needs, and we are willing to seek a solution that serves everyone. By offering choices that are all acceptable to us, the older child feels like he is being heard and treated fairly. We get to take a deep breath as we finish dinner without threatening or screaming.

Until both children are older, this approach isn't going to end the problem of siblings sharing space and possessions, though it does promote open communication. Demanding that siblings either share or leave each other alone doesn't develop a relationship of empathy and cooperation. Threatening punishment or insisting that the kids are giving you a headache as a way to manipulate them into being peaceful merely creates a veneer of cooperation.

Is your desire to stop the fighting just in the moment? Or is your vision to use this challenge as an opportunity to model peaceful coexistence? You don't always have to put your own needs on hold to give your kids negotiating skills. But if you are willing to see these early battles as teaching moments, you can lay the groundwork for the type of communication that will serve everyone well as the children grow and mature.

As they get older, they will learn that when you are too frazzled to help, they actually have the skills to work an issue out themselves. There will also be moments when the best you can do is suggest they retreat to neutral ground until everyone feels calmer, at which time they can try again. Your consistent patience teaches them to handle their squabbles on their own, without the meanness and teasing that usually accompany sibling rivalry.

You don't have to do this perfectly, and there will be days when it will go smoothly and days when deeper issues may rise to the surface, creating additional emotional chaos. With your leadership, and repeated practice, the family can learn to express their truths in a way that fosters mutual compassion and respect.

CHAPTER 5

EXAMINE YOUR BELIEFS ABOUT PARENTING

"A man is but the product of his thoughts;
what he thinks, he becomes"

— Ghandi

WHAT ARE YOUR CORE BELIEFS?

Science is exploding with new information about the way our subconscious works, often wreaking havoc in our personal lives and our family — and it all goes back to childhood.

Brain research suggests the first five years are crucial for establishing our basic beliefs. Early experiences become the subconscious platform for how we see ourselves in the world, the lens through which all our experiences are perceived. As we watch our parents' reactions, hear their words, and feel their energy, we draw conclusions about the way the world works.

To the degree we as parents are stuck in untested beliefs, we tend to make typical parenting mistakes. To parent powerfully requires us to examine the beliefs we live by so we can change what isn't working in the family. Unless we do so, we limit not only our children but also ourselves. Each of us needs to get in touch with our subconscious beliefs about our worthiness, relationships, health, money, success, fear, and worry. This is what determines our parenting style, forever affecting our relationship with our children.

We may think we are parenting from a loving concern that our children will grow into good human beings. We may tell ourselves the choices we make are because we want the best for them. However, my research indicates that much of our behavior stems from unconscious factors that aren't even in the vicinity of love.

Every culture and family has at its core a set of beliefs. This ingrained way of thinking becomes our norm, so that contrary ideas may feel uncomfortable, disrespectful, and even disloyal. Children learn that to be good, they must adapt to the beliefs their family bequeaths to them.

Some of these beliefs are:

- Don't question authority.
- Listen to your elders.
- Do as you are told.
- Make other people happy.
- If you don't learn it now, you'll never learn it.

If we want to parent with the genius we possess, we have to be honest with ourselves, becoming aware of the beliefs that drive our relationship with our children. How true are the beliefs we hold?

Working from the examples listed above, do you really believe children shouldn't question authority? If so, how is a child to learn the difference between blind obedience and respectful disagreement?

Do you really believe that children should always listen to their elders? What if the older person is irresponsible, emotionally unstable, or a pedophile? If they should always listen to their elders, how is a child to learn the difference between respect and being forced to do something that doesn't feel right?

Do you really want your children to always do as they are told? If so, how is your child to juggle all the different things they are told to do throughout the day, some of which may be conflicting? And what should your child do when they receive mixed messages from different authority figures?

Parenting power isn't aimed at getting our children to listen to us. It springs from self-awareness, which in turn allows our children to see us as authentic role models.

THE PART YOUR SUBCONSCIOUS
PLAYS IN PARENTING

When we were little, we each did many things that concerned, worried, irritated, and frustrated our parents. There was nothing wrong with us — we were doing what kids do. We also did many things that brought our parents delight. The messages we received from their responses to our behavior contributed to the beliefs we unconsciously take into our own parenting journey. We learned to give meaning to events that in reality had no meaning. If our parents repeatedly told us we were lazy or naughty because we didn't put our toys away, or that we were good because we did put our toys away, they imparted to us a belief about ourselves. However, in reality, toys scattered around a room have *no* inherent value, positive or negative. They only hold the meaning we give them.

The issue isn't whether toys should be put away, but the message children receive about their worthiness as the parent attempts to get the room tidy. Naturally, we like our children's rooms to be organized. But that's a practical matter. The difference between feeling either empowered or a victim lies in the *meaning* we give to what are in reality nothing more than practical matters.

In so many cases our parents loved us very much, but they weren't aware of the repercussions of their spoken and unspoken messages. Past generations didn't take time to reflect on the way their messages were interpreted. In contrast, empowered parents are aware that belief systems are being created during the seemingly insignificant moments of daily living. They realize that children are literal and don't understand intention, which means we have to be extremely mindful of what we say.

Let's look more closely at some of the messages children receive. Perhaps you were told, "You are such a good child. You make daddy so proud. I can always count on you." If you received this type of message, what belief did it create in you? I suggest it was something like this: "I am good. I do the right things. I make people happy. I'm the favorite. I'm loved. I make my Dad happy. I need to always be responsible and never disappoint anyone."

If you received messages that were negative, they may have sounded like:

- What's wrong with you?
- How many times do I have to tell you the same thing?
- Why can't you be more like your brother?
- You just love to aggravate me.
- You're too sensitive for your own good.
- You would do better if you weren't so lazy.
- I'll do that for you because you don't know how to do it the right way.
- You'll never amount to anything.

If you received such messages, what beliefs did they create in you? Most likely something like, "I'm worthless. Nothing I do is ever good enough. No one notices me when I'm good — they only see what I do wrong. Life isn't fair. It's my fault my Dad is always angry. There must be something wrong with me."

Some messages are indirect, coming from a parent's facial

expression, body language, or energy. If your mom's face lit up every time you walked into the room, you may have created a belief about yourself that says, "I bring joy. People like to be with me." If your dad's face often had a scowl, you may have created a belief that says, "Life isn't safe. I have to stay vigilant to protect myself." If your parents turned away from you when they were angry, disappointed, or annoyed, you may have created a story that says, "I'm really alone. I can't depend on anyone loving me. I must please others if I want to belong."

In addition to verbal and nonverbal messages, parents who continually rescue their child from the sting of a poor decision send the message that the child isn't strong enough to deal with consequences, which can lead to the child feeling helpless. It's important that children experience the consequences of their actions, which are fundamentally different from punishment. Consequences aren't something we "decide on" or "give" a child, but the effects that emerge naturally from their actions.

Throughout our growing years, we experienced a variety of circumstances that continued to fill in our belief system. If our parents had unrealistic expectations, were immature or emotionally unhealthy, used guilt, shame, or sarcasm, or simply didn't understand what children need in order to develop their intellectual, emotional, social, and spiritual potential, we may have received messages that morphed into limiting beliefs.

None of this is about judging our parents. I don't know any parent who intentionally instills limiting beliefs in their children. It happens unconsciously, and it takes awareness to avoid the trap of sending unhealthy messages.

The parents I've worked with have helped me develop a list of limiting core beliefs. You may resonate with some of these:

- I'm not good enough. Nothing I do will ever be enough.
- I can't bear making mistakes.
- People are out to get me.
- Money is the indicator of my success.
- I have to prove to my parents that I'm worthy of their love.
- I'm not outgoing enough.
- Sickness is all around me. I must be vigilant against germs.
- I'm responsible for the happiness of others.
- I need the approval of others.
- I'm not as good as they think I am.
- I'm a fraud.
- Nothing goes right for me.
- I must never show my true feelings.
- I can't trust people; I'm on my own.
- If they knew the real me, they would be disappointed.

A belief is a statement about reality that we have come to think of as true. Although a belief isn't a feeling, it seems to take hold at our gut level, owning space within us. Once attached to our identity, it requires conscious attention to determine how a belief is either working for us or against us. Someone may try to talk us out of the belief, but we are so attached to it that it "feels" like we must hold onto it. We can't shake the sense there's some truth to it.

When I was a little girl, I got the message it was my job to make other people happy. I felt safe when I received approval from my family and teachers. It seemed important to me to have the approval of the bus driver, the postman, and the clerk in the grocery store. I knew I was adored, but with this adoration came conditions. I had to be a good girl and never disappoint my elders.

When I was two years old, my parents divorced and my dad disappeared from my life, so my mom and I moved in with my grandparents. No one explained where my dad went. When children don't receive age-appropriate explanations, they create their own "truth" in their thoughts. I told myself, "My daddy must have gone away because I was bad. I don't know what I did wrong, but I don't want my mommy or grandma to go away, so I always have to be good."

My grandma was like a second mother to me. I loved how it felt to be cherished by her. I remember how painful it was at those moments when she withdrew her love, either with an angry facial expression or dismissive body language. Though she was my greatest cheerleader and I always knew I could go to her for love and support, I also knew there was an unspoken expectation to behave a certain way. My grandma's messages, coupled with the story I created in my young head, gave birth to the limiting belief that to feel safe, I needed the approval of others.

Once limiting beliefs become part of our identity, they feel like a normal way of being. Even when they are negative, confusing, or conflicting, we adopt them so deeply that they are difficult to erase. Nevertheless, if we want to be an empowered parent, we must muster the courage to examine our beliefs and shift them so we don't pass them on to our children.

I actually did pass on some of my limiting "good girl" beliefs to my son Matthew. When he was four years old, I thought it would be a good idea to make a play date with a friend from his nursery school class. I asked his teacher who Matthew liked to play with. She looked at me and said, "I don't think you're going to like my answer." She went on to say that Matthew liked to hang out with the worst behaved boy in the class. She explained that she believed it was because he was living vicariously through the "naughty" behavior of the other child. Matt never got into trouble himself, though he seemed to enjoy being close to it.

I came to see that because Matthew was such an easygoing little boy, he received messages from me affirming how "good" he was. This put pressure on him to keep up his "good boy" image. On many occasions as he was growing up, I noticed how clever he was at teasing his sister and getting a rise out of her while looking puzzled, as if he had no idea why she was carrying on. He learned how to look good in the eyes of adults, while becoming adept at being mischievous in a sneaky way.

I unconsciously passed on the belief to Matthew that to continue to receive my love, he had to be "good." It took his nursery school teacher to help me realize I had to lighten up and allow Matt to be a little bit naughty. By releasing my own past programming I gave permission to myself, as well as my children, not to have to be perfect to be worthy of love.

RELEASE YOUR PAST PROGRAMMING

There are two important reasons to uncover and release our limiting beliefs. The first is because they affect our sense of worthiness, happiness, confidence, and contentment. When we feel worthy and optimistic, we handle our challenges with ease and flow. Our child's behavior isn't interpreted as a direct attack on our personhood. We are able to connect with our calmest, clearest, highest self. In contrast, when we feel less hopeful, less worthy, victimized, or fearful, we handle challenges from a sense of lack, stress, or angst. With a head full of thoughts based on limiting beliefs, we are more apt to yell, threaten, explode, shame, spank, or give in to our children.

The second reason to uncover and release our limiting beliefs is that unless we have addressed our own unresolved emotional issues, we unwittingly fall into typical parenting traps that stem from such baggage. Many parents give more thought to their child's physical world than they do to their child's inner world, even though the inner landscape is where the most important growth is taking place. However, we can't understand the power of a child's thoughts, beliefs, and emotions until we do inner work ourselves.

Our own behavior is the indicator we need to release limiting beliefs. While most parents worry to a degree and periodically feel unappreciated, the intensity of these feelings determines whether our beliefs are interfering with our parenting. If we find ourselves yelling, threatening, punishing, or giving in, we have work to do on ourselves.

Our mother may believe that a good parent worries about their children. Our father may argue that a spank on the rear end isn't harmful. Our sister may insist that timeout is the best way get children to listen. As we reflect on our beliefs and listen to the messages from our own inner wisdom, we may find we want to parent differently from our family and friends. It isn't about "being right," but about taking ourselves to our highest place of integrity, learning how to engage children in cooperative, respectful behavior, and parenting with wisdom and compassion.

Most of us believe our children's behavior causes us grief and worry. However, once we realize that parenting begins in our own mind, we cease giving so much energy to trying to control our kids and turn inward to where our power resides. We realize that many of our beliefs actually cause our children to live in fear, acquiescing rather than learning communication skills, and confusing love with control.

When my children were in elementary school, I continued unraveling my limiting beliefs. My husband was in charge of dinner on those days when I taught late into the evening. I remember driving down the street to our house feeling exhausted but excited to see the family I adored. When I walked into the messy kitchen, my feelings quickly turned to anger. Three jackets were hanging on the backs of three kitchen chairs. Dishes were piled in the sink and the table was covered with crumbs and dirty napkins. This wasn't the first time the cleanup crew had gone missing. My husband and children were sitting in front of the television, oblivious of the mess. I was so upset, I didn't welcome the children's hugs and didn't want a kiss from my husband. I wanted a clean kitchen!

The thoughts that swirled through my mind went something like, "No one appreciates how hard I work. My husband should be a role model and not hang his coat on a chair. Why doesn't anyone around here listen to me? No one cares how I feel. If they loved me, they wouldn't leave such a mess."

Do you hear the deeply ingrained limiting belief that was driving my anger? "If they loved me, they would change their behavior so I would feel good." This belief had been handed down from my beloved grandmother, who taught me that when you love someone, you behave in ways that make the person happy.

It took many conversations with a wise friend for me to realize that this limiting belief was at the root of feeling unloved. At first I was unwilling to change because I believed all the arguments were on my side: Shouldn't the people who love you care how you feel and want you to be happy? What's the big deal to change your behavior if it makes the person you love feel better?

Entrenched as this thinking was, none of it actually felt good. It also clouded the way I acted toward my husband and children. I wanted to love them with unbounded energy, but I felt restricted because underlying every joyful moment was the thought that they didn't really care about me.

After several weeks of feeling miserable, I became willing to turn my thoughts around. I allowed myself to try thinking a new set of truths:

- My family's behavior isn't a reflection of their love for me.
- I can choose to feel loved, even with a dirty kitchen.
- I can communicate my needs in a more effective, less emotional way.
- There's no one right solution. There are choices. I could give up my late-night teaching and the extra income.
- No one is responsible for my happiness but me.

Once I was aware of my limiting beliefs, I learned how to communicate my needs clearly and honestly, without judgment, hysteria, or imposing guilt. I requested a family meeting in which I explained, "When I see dirty dishes and coats thrown on chairs, I feel irritated because I like to come home to a clean and orderly kitchen. Would you be willing to straighten up the kitchen before watching television? I'm also thinking about giving up my evening teaching so I can be home to help with the evening routines."

We came up with a solution that respected everyone's needs. My family took responsibility for cleaning the kitchen after watching a limited amount of television. I wasn't expected to help and could take a relaxing shower while they finished their chores. I learned to appreciate their efforts and relax my high expectations. Most important of all, I let go of my belief that their behavior was an indicator of their love.

The ability to live as an empowered parent emerges when we uncover the beliefs that are driving our behavior. Once we are clear about the deeper layers that complicate our interactions, we can observe ourselves to see whether our actions are producing healthy results. As we do so, we become aware of the messages we are *actually* giving our children, not the messages we *wish* we were giving them. It doesn't matter that our intentions are positive. What matters is that we are honest with ourselves, so that our delivery is healthy.

CHAPTER 6

AUTHENTIC PARENTING BEGINS WITH BEING HONEST WITH YOURSELF

"Your mind is right now filled with old thoughts. Not only old thoughts, but mostly someone else's old thoughts. It's important now, it's time now, to change your mind about some things."

— Neale Donald Walsch

A SENSE OF SELF

To be human means to have a sense of self. This helps us make decisions, maintain self-esteem, set boundaries, and strive for higher awareness. When we have a healthy sense of self, we can afford to reflect on our thoughts and emotions, take responsibility for our behavior, and be sensitive to the people and creatures that share our world, instead of feeling defensive.

A healthy sense of self is the source of a sense of personal power. When we operate from such a state, we are compassionate rather than judgmental, seeing challenges as opportunities for growth rather than excuses for feeling like a victim. Mistakes become the bedrock of growth instead of indicators of failure. While we take joyful pride in our accomplishments, we don't measure our worth by the accolades or criticism we receive from others.

Without being aware of it, we often operate from an egoic state, which is fundamentally different from having a healthy sense of self. The unchecked ego shows itself when a parent becomes overly critical, controlling, hovering, or excusing. In an attempt to soothe fears or make sure our dreams for the future come true, we may continually point out where our children need to improve. Some parents become overly involved in feathering their child's nest, ensuring that all goes smoothly for them.

The ego makes judgments and assigns labels. We may not be

able to feel genuinely happy for another child's accomplishments, and we may be oblivious of the way we are critical of others. From the triumphs of potty training to landing the lead in a play, we may find ourselves competing with others. Whenever we feel better about ourselves by judging, criticizing, or comparing, we are likely operating from an egoic state.

While it can be challenging to define the boundary between confidence and grandiosity, it may be helpful to think about the difference between experiencing joyful pride versus competitive bragging. The following are examples of parenting from an unchecked ego:

- Becoming righteous toward parents who are struggling with an issue we have dealt with successfully.

- Comparing our children with other children as a way of evaluating how well we are doing.

- Exaggerating, bragging, being competitive.

- Our adult decisions constantly trump our children's needs, requiring them to continually adjust to our demands.

- Being unwilling to change our behavior and expecting our child to simply listen and fall in line.

- Expecting our child to change their perspective just because we are bigger and older.

- Shaping our child according to our wishes and aspirations, not their own inherent blueprint.

- Viewing our child's mistakes and accomplishments as a reflection of our own status.

- Insisting on a particular college or career path because anything less would be unacceptable or embarrassing.

AUTHENTIC PARENTING POWER

Parenting from an egoic state leads to actions that trigger power struggles, rebellion, and the shutting down of feelings in our children. When a parent operates from this part of their makeup, they are looking at reality through a veil of deception.

COME OUT FROM BEHIND YOUR MASK

Losing connection with our authentic self happens so unconsciously that we aren't even aware it's happening. Once we lack an authentic sense of self, an egoic mask takes over, enabling us to feel safe as we interact with others. What we don't realize is that our mask also blinds us to our insecurities.

Whenever we wear masks of success, respectability, perfection, happiness, generosity, or belonging, we tend to react impulsively and lose our ability to truly be helpful to our children. We may have a prestigious job, a beautiful house, a fancy car, and all the trappings of success, but because of our impoverished sense of self we still need our child to bring home a grade that makes us look good.

The following are examples of how egoic masks show up in our parenting style:

- Having to be right.
- Defending our position.
- Criticizing and blaming others.
- Judging and labeling.
- Worrying about the future.
- Bringing up past hurt.
- Needing to look good in the eyes of others — a form of

false pride.

- Taking things personally.

When we are unaware of our authentic self and instead parent from an egoic state, it tends to sound like this:

- "Make me proud."
- "Be a good boy and give me a kiss."
- "Didn't I just tell you not to do that?"
- " I'm the boss."
- "Because I said so."
- "You're an embarrassment to the family."
- "Children in my house don't behave like that."
- "There are no crybabies in this home."
- "Other kids can do it. What's wrong with you?"
- "What will other people think?"
- "How do you think that makes me look?"

Emotional well-being, sustained happiness, and relationship building are a direct effect of identifying and removing our egoic masks. The only thing we have to lose in this process is the pain of never really connecting with our children and wondering why our relationship with them is struggling.

WHY YOU SHOULD ENGAGE IN SELF-REFLECTION

Earlier, I talked about the need for self-reflection. Many parents resist self-reflection. Their ego kicks in and screams, "This is the way I parent. I don't need anyone to tell me to do it differently. My kids have to learn I know what's best for them. I'm the parent, and they have to respect me. This is the way my parents did it, and I turned out just fine."

Other parents say there's no time in their busy lives to engage in self-reflection. Telling ourselves we don't have time is one of the cunning ways the ego deceives. If we have time to shop on the internet, watch television, or use a phone app, then there's time to reflect. The issue isn't time, but willingness. The ego is terrified of transformation. Self-reflection means we may have to change our entrenched ways of behaving.

Even the busiest parent can self-reflect during the ride home from work, while exercising, walking, taking a shower, or snuggling under the covers after a busy day. Meditation is a particularly wonderful tool for quieting the mind and listening to the wisdom that pours forth from our soul. Find what works for you and dedicate yourself to a regular routine. Taking time to reflect on your egoic mask has the power to alter the quality of the relationships in your life.

It's important to understand that guilt is never part of authentic self-reflection. On the contrary, self-reflection is an act of loving ourselves, so that we learn from our mistakes. The difference between a mistake and a learning opportunity is whether we grow from the experience. A mistake may be thought of as a mis-take, as in not seizing the growth opportunity inherent in an experience. When we reflect on our behavior from a place of self-love, we have an opportunity to learn how to do things differently next time. By letting go of self-judgment and our need to perform perfectly, we become more willing to do the same for the people closest to us — our children and our parenting partner.

Once we begin to self-reflect, we find we can more readily rein in a reaction in a challenging moment. Even if we lose ourselves by beginning to threaten or yell because our buttons have been pushed, we can quickly regain our sanity and move into our power by using what I call a "pivoting" strategy.

To illustrate what I mean by a pivoting strategy, consider a dad who attended my classes and began to routinely reflect on the way he handled his children's unpleasant behavior. As his reflection deepened, he became increasingly aware that if his day had been stressful, he wasn't going to be on top of his game and needed to be especially aware of this.

One evening when he walked into the house after a hard day and discovered toys and board game pieces all over the living room floor, he found himself triggered and began to scream at his kids, aged four and six, telling them they couldn't watch television that evening. Upon hearing their punishment, the children began sobbing, blaming each other. Said the dad, if the mess wasn't cleaned up immediately there would be no television for the rest of the week. When his wife came downstairs to see what all the fuss was about, he also lashed out at her, accusing her of allowing the children to be spoiled and irresponsible.

He described what happened next: "I suddenly had the thought to stop and just breathe. It was as if I was outside my body watching myself. My face felt distorted and my heart was hard. I became willing to stop yelling and just kept breathing. I could feel my stress start to subside and sense my heart was softening. My angry thoughts shifted to loving thoughts. I realized the children didn't purposely aggravate me. I sensed this was a big moment in my relationship with my kids. I had an opportunity to model blame, rage, and powerlessness, or communicate in a way that would plant seeds of trust, appreciation, and love. I put up my hand and gently said, 'Stop. I want to stop. Rewind. Start again.' I asked my wife and kids to come sit on the couch and looked into their eyes. I told them how awful it felt to come home after a busy day and find their mess. I acknowledged they didn't intend to add more stress to my life, and my reaction came swiftly and powerfully. I acknowledged that no television was a punishment that just spilled out and that it was more important for us to learn from this than for anyone to get punished. I hoped they could find a way to talk about what really happened without a need to blame each other. We cleaned up the room together and gave each other 'high fives.' In the days that followed there was an easy spirit of cooperation in the house. The kids were proud of themselves as they remembered to get things done without reminders. While I would have liked this change to be permanent I knew that I had to continue to work on my reactive nature in order to bring out the best in them."

Miracles do indeed occur when we use such a self-reflective pivoting technique to return to a connected state.

HOW TO DELIBERATELY SHIFT
YOUR THOUGHTS

If we aren't aware of our thoughts, or are convinced we are correct in our thinking, we risk parenting from an emotionally unhealthy state. For instance, if we entertain fearful thoughts, we are likely to generate fear in our children. Similarly, mental stress results in stressed behavior. Thoughts based in anger, defiance, jealously, disempowerment, or judgment make their way into the messages we directly and indirectly give our kids.

Whether or not we are aware we have these thoughts, they nevertheless affect our children, since our children are always watching us. It isn't our words that shape them, but how we live our life. For example, we may scream at our children because they are arguing with each other, demanding they learn to get along. If we don't model the behavior we expect from our children, our children detect our hypocrisy. Then we wonder why, when they are teenagers, they roll their eyes at us.

While it isn't always easy to shift the thinking that leads us to feel worried, guilty, unworthy, jealous, angry, blaming, disappointed, or overwhelmed, we have the ability to change limiting thought patterns and move into a state of authentic power.

You become a deliberate thinker when you start to notice your negative thoughts throughout the day. If you are used to giving more attention to the limiting thoughts that tend to make you feel like a victim, focusing on fear and lack, it's time to exchange such thoughts for the kind of thoughts that will tend to open you up, generating more hopeful, positive expectations, and shining a spotlight on a way of seeing things you may not have entertained before. The focus shifts from what's wrong with our lives, including our children, to empowering thoughts that not only cause us to feel better but also lead to better parenting choices.

You can begin the shifting process by noticing your thoughts as you move through the day. Pay attention to the way you interpret your world. Here are some examples of limiting thoughts versus empowering thoughts:

LIMITING THOUGHTS

- "People are so selfish."
- "It's a tough world."
- "Work is no fun."
- "What a jerk!"
- "I'll never get through this."
- "Life is unfair."
- "Their behavior is an embarrassment."
- "No one ever listens to me."
- "They'll never amount to anything."
- "I can't be happy until things change around here."

EMPOWERING THOUGHTS

- "There are some really wonderful people out there."
- "Everyone sees things from their own perspective."
- "Things have a way of always working out."
- "It's amazing how many good things have come my way."
- "External accomplishments don't indicate internal contentment."
- "I can find something to think about that makes me happy in this very moment."

When we get into the habit of shifting the way we perceive our experiences, opportunities to get out of the rut defined by our old story and onto a new pathway of possibilities emerge. Here are some examples of how it's done:

"People are so selfish, only out for themselves."

becomes

"Actually there are many people who are kind. I've been with people who can get their own needs met while being thoughtful of others. I've encountered some really caring folks."

"It's a tough world. Work is overwhelming; I can't bear it. Life is so unfair."

becomes

"Life has lots of challenges. It's amazing how many good things have actually come my way. I'll put this challenge in perspective. I can figure something out."

"What a jerk. He always says something stupid."

becomes

"I wonder what he was thinking. I wonder if something big is going on inside him."

"Her behavior is outrageous. I can't put up with this for another minute. If she doesn't get her act together, she'll never amount to anything."

becomes

"It's pretty normal for kids to go through these crises. There's a huge growing opportunity here. I wonder what she needs from me in order to move through this difficult time?"

Whenever we react to our children by snapping, yelling, threatening, or punishing, we are allowing ourselves to believe our child's behavior is fueling the conflict, whereas in reality it's often our thoughts. Stuck in habits of thinking that don't serve our family well, we need to take a step toward greater awareness. The following questions are designed to foster increased awareness in any situation:

- What makes me sure that what I believe about my child's behavior is true? Is it from observing other people's experiences, bombardment from the media, or a message ingrained in me when I was a child?

- Could there be another way of thinking about this? Am I willing to shift my thoughts?

- Would I feel better, lighter, happier if I took a different approach?

- Would I act differently with my children if I thought about them in a new way?

- What would change in my relationship with my children if I started to think and respond differently?

Letting go of deeply ingrained beliefs can feel like we are losing a piece of ourselves. Who would we be were we to relax our hold on the thoughts at the base of our behavior? I can tell you what's waiting for you if you take such a step: the ability to engage in close, connected relationships with your children.

When we constantly tell ourselves stories in our head, we think they are the whole truth, whereas they are often merely our flawed perceptions. We give meaning to a situation based on our temperament, early conditioning, unconscious programming, and ego.

HOW SHIFTING YOUR THOUGHTS
WORKS IN PRACTICE

Let me conclude this chapter by sharing with you four different situations in which parents were able to change their thinking, and as a result witnessed huge shifts in their child's behavior.

The first case is that of twenty-one-month-old Michael, whose mother became concerned when, as she tried to console him after he fell down, he bit her and slapped the sleeping baby in her arms. "I know he's a good boy," she told me, "but I just don't know how to handle his 'terrible twos.'"

As we talked, it emerged that Michael had a new baby sister. At his stage of development, biting is a behavior to be expected, especially given that Michael's temperament was one of easily feeling frustrated. The addition of a baby sister created the perfect set of circumstances to trigger biting.

Understanding this altered how Michael's mother and father perceived his behavior. Taking all judgment out of their thoughts and language, they began to respond to him from the insight that biting isn't about being good or bad, and neither is this stage of development terrible. Michael wasn't either testing or manipulating, but was experiencing a legitimate internal struggle. Once his parents ceased worrying something was wrong with him, they were able to alter the energy with which they approached him. Whenever he became frustrated and bit or hit, his mother acknowledged his feelings while also consistently setting limits: "It is OK to be angry. It is not OK to hit because hitting hurts. I think you want to tell me something." (Mom also realized she needed to read his signals so she could attend to him before his frustration led to biting.)

The temptation in such situations is to punish. However, punishment is not only ineffective but tends to intensify the anger a child is feeling. In contrast to punishment, the *natural consequence* of biting and hitting is that you don't want to be close to a child if they are going to bite or hit. The key is to move away physically, while being extremely careful not to withdraw your love.

When adults respond calmly, without giving the child too much attention, the child learns to express angry feelings in a constructive manner. This is an opportunity for the parents to be self-reflective concerning how they express their own frustration and anger. They can be effective role models by saying, "I feel angry right now," without acting out. In this way the child learns that angry feelings are valid, though not to be acted upon. To prevent misbehavior, a parent can anticipate situations in which a child will likely experience frustration and either stand by to make sure nobody gets hurt or calmly and lovingly remove the child from the scene.

It's also important to acknowledge a child's progress, noticing when they do things well and talking openly about their feelings. In Michael's case, although he was the "big brother," it was important for his parents to keep in mind that he was still very young and needed lots of their time and positive attention.

In another situation, Caroline's professionally successful mother was constantly engaged in power struggles with her strongly opinionated four-year-old daughter. Everything seemed to involve a battle of wills. With a few coaching sessions, the mother realized her belief that a child should listen because a parent ought to be respected was fueling the battles. She admitted she didn't enjoy spending time playing with her child and often wondered why she gave in to the pressure of becoming a mom. Once she became willing to allow Caroline more choices throughout the day and began giving her pleasurable attention, the power struggles were greatly reduced.

We come now to eight-year-old Ryan, who loved playing video games and loathed eating vegetables, which triggered threats from his dad to ban his electronic games. I asked the father whether he was willing to shift his thinking, and he agreed to try another approach. Dad made a conscious effort to give positive attention to Ryan for two weeks, asking about his favorite video game and saying nothing about uneaten vegetables. He then invited Ryan to do the weekly food shopping, and together they chose fresh fruits and vegetables. Each day they prepared a new dish together. Ryan actually ate and enjoyed three of them and asked if he and his dad could do it again. The miracle in this is not only that Ryan shifted his eating habits, but that he and his dad connected in a way that strengthened their relationship.

Finally, let me tell you about fourteen-year-old Lisa, who woke up in a grouchy mood and was rude to her mother. The mom's initial reaction was to interpret her daughter's sullenness as disrespectful. About to retort, "What's wrong with you?" she caught herself, choosing instead not to take her daughter's behavior personally. Pivoting mentally, mom told herself, "Something must be feeling off for her. I can be supportive by not reacting." To offer compassion instead of judgment required the mother to tolerate her own discomfort. She then asked her daughter, "Do you need time alone? Something doesn't seem to feel right with you." This small but powerful act of respectfully acknowledging her daughter's need for privacy created the spark of trust that allowed Lisa to come out of her room and give her mom a hug.

Despite these wonderful stories of success as a result of changing our thinking as parents, an earnest desire to move past early programming sometimes isn't enough to alter our thought patterns. As we will see in the next chapter, the latest brain research reveals the hidden factors that control our resistance to making the changes we need to make.

CHAPTER 7

THE ANSWERS LIE IN YOUR BRAIN

"The moment you change your perception is the moment you rewrite the chemistry of your body."

— Dr. Bruce H Lipton

BELIEFS CREATE PATHWAYS

If you have ever tried to drop an entrenched thought and replace it with another, you've likely discovered it can be difficult. The reason is that the more we think in a certain way, the more deeply ingrained our established thought pathways become. Consequently many of our thoughts and much of our behavior are on autopilot. Synapses established through years of conditioning form the neural pathways that automatically become our response in the present moment.

Limiting beliefs create deep grooves in our cellular memory. Since beliefs are strengthened with repetition, our earliest interpretations of experiences created a powerful operating system that unconsciously drives our grownup thoughts.

Because our parenting genius is locked inside the brain's pathways, it's crucial to break the unconscious habits that have hijacked our brain patterns. Today we know this is possible. Neuroscientists are reporting that, with determination, this complex wiring can be reworked. They have learned that the brain is constantly rewiring itself, not only in childhood but also throughout our life as we respond to our feelings, thoughts, and experiences.

Our thoughts actually shape the structure and function of the brain, so that each time we have an experience, the brain makes a connection. A new neural connection repeated over and over creates deeper and deeper pathways in the brain. Every time we use one of these new pathways, it increases the likelihood we'll use them even more.

With both self-awareness and dedicated practice, we can help our brain fire up a new way of being. If we discover habits of thinking or behaving that don't serve us well, we can rewire the pathways that have taken years to develop. However, the deeper our thoughts are etched into our neural circuits, the more conscious we must be in order to embrace another state of mind.

Our task is to compassionately push through the habits of thinking that have already been established in our own brain, while becoming mindful of the ways we are presently contributing to our children's perceptions and thought patterns.

MASTER YOUR OWN MIND

Thoughts are just a creation of our mind. We run into difficulty when we aren't willing to examine the possibility that not all our thoughts are truth. Parents who insist their way is the "right" way and who buy into strict strategies of discipline to enforce their will become prisoners of their own minds.

When we choose to abandon the old paradigm that says children must submit to the "wisdom" of adults, life doesn't become a free-for-all without guiding principles. Rather, we realize a wise parent is constantly learning and growing. We become a master at wondering about the inner life of our children, making it a priority to focus on building positive emotional connections with them instead of only asking questions like how we can get them to listen when we tell them to do something.

New thinking circuits begin to develop when we regularly ask ourselves, "Do I know this child? Do I really see them? Do I hear them? Do I remind them what a gift they are in my life? How do I connect with them? How does my own behavior impact our relationship?" The more we adopt an inquiring approach, the more open we become to inspired decisions on issues such as how to handle a messy room, unfinished homework, or time spent on video games. When we make behavior, not connection, our top priority, kids push back, lie, rebel, experience headaches, become depressed, or start hanging out with the wrong crowd. We think the problem is with them, but research shows their behavior is often the result of how adults approach them. This can be hard for parents to hear, but it's at the heart of much family suffering.

Making *connection* instead of *discipline* the basis of our parenting honors both the parents' and child's sacred journeys. Far from meaning children run wild or are allowed to act irresponsibly, connection increases the potential for raising human beings who are happy, respectful, self-disciplined, and confident. Such children are more likely to become adults who have integrity, enjoy their work and thrive in their relationships.

To illustrate how to connect in a way that honors each individual, take the case of a couple walking down the street hand in hand. As they pass a boutique, the woman pulls the man over to the window and exclaims, "Look at that beautiful red dress. I would love to have that."

The man feels a tightening in his stomach and says, "Another dress? You don't need any more clothes. Did you see the price tag on that dress? You know I can't afford to buy you something like that."

The woman lets go of his hand and questions whether she picked the right partner. The man scowls, feels unappreciated, and wonders how such a lovely evening suddenly turned so cold.

Let's give the story a different ending. When the woman expresses a desire to have such a beautiful dress, the man feels tension in his stomach but this time chooses to soothe himself instead of reacting. Then from a place of calmness he says, "And you would be the most beautiful woman who ever wore that dress. One day, I want to be able to buy you something just like that."

The woman snuggles closer to the man, certain she picked the right partner. The man feels wonderful and looks forward to the rest of the evening.

In neither version of the story does the woman get the dress. The difference lies in the fact the woman felt heard instead of judged. She didn't need the dress in order to feel happy or loved. She simply needed to feel *heard*.

In the first version of the story, the man couldn't see his part in the fact the evening took a negative turn. This is also the case in many of our interactions with our children. Youngsters don't learn when we demand they stop wanting things. They learn when they feel heard, which reassures them they are worthy.

When a specific *behavior* isn't our focus, but rather our child's sense of well-being, we handle situations entirely differently. For instance, when a child asks for a cookie, begs for his own iPhone, or demands to be treated like an adult, it's helpful to remember that the most important thing is to first soothe ourselves. This allows us to respond constructively instead of reacting negatively. We handle the immediate situation effectively, while at the same time developing a bond that will mature with trust and affection.

As our children receive repeated meaningful affirmation, they learn life is sweetest not when they get everything they think they must have but when they master their emotions, think positively, and engage in healthy relationships. Through repeated experiences of feeling worthy, they develop a confidence that life will generally work out well for them.

Parents want to know how to deal with specific behaviors: How do I get my child to stop coming into our bed at night? How do I get my kids to be nice to each other? How do I get my child to be more responsible? Since each child is different, rarely is there a simple answer.

The red dress story may seem a bit simplistic in terms of the more complex challenges parents face. For instance, what do you do after you lovingly say, "You wish you could have that cookie, and you can after dinner," and your child throws a tantrum? What do you do when you've reminded your child to do their homework, but you find them playing games on the computer? How do you respond when you find out your teenager has lied about where they were the previous evening?

Despite its simplicity, the red dress story points the way. First, you soothe yourself. Next, you honor your child's experiences, perceptions, and emotions. It doesn't matter that you may not agree and see things differently. It matters only that they feel heard and understood. This puts you in a place to move forward with a plan of action that honors your own integrity and your child's dignity.

HOW TO CHANGE YOUR BRAIN PATTERNS

Scientists can now explain why the red dress approach is so effective and why, in contrast, it's so compromising for the brain to think negative thoughts. We understand for the first time in history why it's unhealthy for our children to be disciplined using threats, guilt, shame, or some form of punishment.

Our understanding of how the brain develops reveals that a child's brain simply isn't capable of interpreting our anger, indifference, judgments, threats, or sarcasm as forms of caring. For the brain to develop pathways of feeling loved, it must experience love. This is why there's such power in questioning the truth of our ingrained beliefs about bringing children up. When we do so, our children begin to experience us differently, in our fundamentally loving self.

How can we initiate the process of changing our brain patterns? Let me share with you four steps:

1. Lovingly and courageously watch yourself.

- Be aware of your inner dialogue and the conversations in your head. What are you telling yourself about your children, their choices, their behavior, and your relationship with them? Are you positive that in order to be a good parent, you must worry or demand they do as they are told?

- Notice how often you think habitual thoughts. Are they based on fear or optimism? How do you feel after you think these thoughts? Why are you resistant to changing your thoughts?

- Mentally step outside your body and observe your behavior. How do you react when your child does something that annoys you? Notice what triggers you. Is any of it coming from your own stressful thoughts?

2. Question yourself and be open to wondering.

• How did your thoughts and behavior become your truth? Are you replicating your parents' beliefs? Are you copying your friends? Are you influenced by the media? Have you done your own solid research on how children learn and develop?

• Are you willing to entertain different possibilities? Are you ready to do more research or take a parenting class? Have you worked through your own childhood issues?

• How might you feel if you shifted some of your thinking and reacting? Would you relax, worry less, and lighten up?

3. Commit to change.

• Ask yourself whether your relationship with your children is worth examining your beliefs. For example, a recurrent thought might be, "My life is too stressful to be more patient with the children."

• Are you willing to give up being "right" in order to have a better relationship?

• Wonder out loud what you can do to interrupt your established patterns of thinking and reacting.

• Partner with someone you trust to help you be accountable for continuing this self-examination.

4. Beyond parenting.

• Stay conscious of your repetitive patterns of thinking, feeling, and behaving in all areas of your life. This will enable you to see how fear and negativity spill over into your interactions with your children.

- Be aware of any self-defeating habits already ingrained in your brain circuitry. Notice when your thoughts are driven by a sense of inadequacy, a belief you don't deserve success, or a feeling of not being seen or heard, not belonging, or not feeling lovable. These may show up at work or in friendships.

- Become honest about your compulsive behavior. If you find yourself needing to overeat, rely on wine or other alcoholic beverages to relieve daily stress, spend money beyond your means, exercise to an extreme, or indulge in any behavior that's having a negative impact on your family, you may want to seek professional support in rewiring some deep neural firing patterns.

YOUR PRIMITIVE BRAIN

A part of the brain called the amygdala is almond-sized and almond-shaped. When I first learned about the function of the amygdala, I was deeply appreciative because it explained so much of the behavior I observed in both children and adults. Millions of nerves connect the amygdala to many of the brain centers, including the neocortex, which is our executive center. The circuitry between the amygdala and the higher-functioning executive center is central to the relationship between emotions, critical thinking, and behavior. Those who work in child development sometimes refer to the amygdala as the reptilian part of the brain. Vital to our survival when, as a species we had to be on constant alert for predators, its most important function was to trigger the fight-or-flight response, which is part of the primitive neural circuitry that kept humans vigilant and therefore alive in dangerous situations.

Even though we now possess a more sophisticated thinking brain, the amygdala remains a powerful force that can't simply be switched to the "off" position. The components of fear go beyond thinking and reasoning. After a frightening experience, we retain the reaction in our brain circuitry. Consequently, when something triggers a memory of the event, our body reacts as if reliving the experience. The emotions associated with such memories are stored in the amygdala.

When we were children, if we felt abandoned or experienced a lack of worthiness or belonging, we stored the fear associated with these experiences in our primitive brain. If we lived in terror of punishment, teasing, or withdrawal of parental approval, we still carry the residual fear in our amygdala. If we lived with parents who were demanding, suffocating, inconsistent, or emotionally distant, we have buried the fear that comes along with those conditions deep within the chemistry of our brain. If we were spanked, hit, and verbally or physically abused, those memories can well up as sensations in our body, so that in an instant it's as if we are right back in our childhood.

Childhood feelings of powerlessness stored in the amygdala fan the outrageous behavior exhibited by many adults. Whenever I observe grownups expressing exaggerated anger or fear and ask about their childhood, we eventually uncover the original source of the behavior, which is generally some type of childhood wound that has created a need to be vigilant, protect themselves, run away, fight back, or shut down.

When we use childhood coping mechanisms in our adult lives, we literally turn ourselves over to our childhood wounds and our primitive brain. The way to break the cycle is to retrain the circuitry. This means moving through our deepest fears.

DON'T MISTAKE FEAR FOR LOVE

The anxiety, frustration, guilt, and huge amount of stress that accompany parenting all originate in fear. Dissolve the fear that permeates so much of the parenting journey, and you begin to experience authentic parenting power. Instead of trying to control the uncontrollable, you find yourself relating to a precious human being as an individual in their own right.

When the overwhelming urge to control gets triggered, it's usually because a fearful thought interrupted our flow of well-being. Fear overshadows our good judgment.

Release any part of your belief system that binds you into acting from fear disguised as love. Breathe out the antiquated ways of parenting that sabotage your joy and your children's joy. Sense your desire to connect with your offspring at the deepest level — the place where your heart, mind, and spirit meet.

If you don't believe fear is a powerful motivator, spend some time observing the ad campaigns that bombard us. It's staggering how many of them are based on fear. Advertisers use fear because fear works.

The problem is that fear isn't the healthiest of motivators. Our body's natural state is one of balance. When a person experiences fear, their primitive brain takes over, pumping out chemicals that limit the functioning of their higher brain — the place where reasoning and intuition live. This is why you don't want to make decisions out of fear, but from your neocortex. Once you are in fear mode, your executive function shuts down and you can't access your wisdom.

The amygdala can be activated by an actual experience, the memory of an experience, or the thought of an experience. When you or your child encounter a fearful, unfamiliar, or unpleasant situation, a chain of events occurs wherein the brain signals the adrenal glands to secrete cortisol. The cortisol alerts the body to release energy for either fighting or fleeing. Cortisol increases heart rate, respiration, and glucose levels, equipping us for fight or flight. Just as we don't control our heartbeat, or even the reflex of blinking, we can't control the automatic release of stress hormones into the bloodstream. Too much cortisol can cause the neocortex to shut down, restricting our ability to think clearly.

If my suggestion that you change the way you think or behave with respect to your children causes you to feel anxious or uncomfortable, your amygdala is likely being triggered. Instead of your higher thinking brain being open to shifting your perspective, the cortisol flowing through your bloodstream puts you on high alert, protecting your ego. This can result in entering a fight, flight, or freeze mode.

In the case of the *fight response*, you may be annoyed at the very suggestion that you should adjust your perspective. You may find yourself becoming defensive or even angry. The more reasons I give you for changing your thoughts, the more angry arguments arise to bolster your existing beliefs. You may try to prove I'm incompetent. If your partner suggested you read this book, you may be furious with them, asserting there's nothing wrong with your parenting skills. To rant and rave as if you are being attacked is a normal adult fight response.

The closer I get to touching your deepest fears, the more likely you are to shift into the *flight response*. You may want to close this book, throw it down, and never look at it again. You may decide I don't know what I'm talking about and declare you don't need help from a so-called expert. If your partner wants to discuss the concepts in this book, you may declare yourself too busy. Your way of handling your discomfort is to flee, going into your cave instead of examining the issues.

There are others who read a book like this and have no reaction, no thoughts in response. They are frozen and therefore can't relate to anything that's said. If you experience the *freeze response*, and your partner asks you what you learned from reading this book, you likely won't be able to remember. In the freeze state, we protect ourselves from feeling threatened by shutting down, locked in a pattern learned in our childhood. Although these states are powerful, we can change any aspect of our parenting style by making a conscious decision to do things differently. Then we must practice, practice, practice, aware that changing patterns takes time.

When we feel safe, sensing we are understood, we are more apt to be open to change. If we feel judged or criticized, we fight, flee, or freeze. Children respond in the same way. Let's take a look at the way it works with our kids.

HOW TO INFLUENCE YOUR CHILD'S BRAIN DEVELOPMENT

Your child's brain is a powerhouse for controlling physiological, emotional, and cognitive functioning. The way you set up your home environment, the messages you offer, and the emotional climate you create impact the chemistry of your child's developing brain.

Data from research in neuroscience shows why we can no longer make excuses for using fear, guilt, shame, rejection, anger, or punishment to control the behavior of our children. Studies show that early experiences with parents or caretakers, together with interaction with the environment, are critical to a child's brain development. Children who live with stress or fear have a much harder time creating the strong, healthy brain connections that enable them to access higher-level thinking — the kind of thinking that allows children to share, control their impulses, make good decisions, transfer information, and understand the consequences of their choices. Higher-level thinking takes place in the frontal lobe of the cerebral neocortex. This center of executive functioning is where motivation, attention, comprehension, and the ability to plan, organize, and solve problems originate.

Many parents expect their children to be capable of executive functioning long before the brain has had ample experiences and opportunities to generate the synapses required to remember and follow through with responsibilities, as well as to share and get along with friends and siblings. The ability to organize homework folders, remember to feed the cat, or be patient with a younger sibling comes with many repeated acts set in an atmosphere of patience, empathy, and appreciation.

Let me share with you what research is showing with regard to negative emotions and brain development:

- When a parent expresses repeated anger toward a child, the child feels a sense of shame and/or fear, creating neurological pathways of unworthiness.

- Children who live in chaotic environments, or who have been hit, severely punished, or have experienced trauma may become hyper vigilant as they stay "on guard" for situations that feel threatening.

• Fear shuts down the thinking part of the brain because the brain focuses on self-protection.

• Self-protection takes place in the emotional center of the brain, the amygdala. This all happens automatically.

In the same way the amygdala activates the body's defense system in adults, it operates full force in children. This explains much of the behavior parents find so frustrating.

With the *fight response*, the child becomes angry, argues, gets defensive, and may become aggressive. The more the parent scolds and the angrier the parent becomes, the more oppositional is the child's response. They may talk back, argue, refuse to obey, scream, or get physical. The child doesn't do this on purpose — it's the automatic reaction of the brain's emotional center.

With the *flight response*, the child tries to get away from the source of fear and shame. They may ignore you, walk or even run away, trying to escape the feeling they are bad. They may cry, whimper, pull something over their head, put their fingers in their ears, or hide. In an attempt to stay safe, they probably won't tell you the truth. Older children may lock their door and not come out of their room. The child isn't manipulating or lying in a planned way, but is reacting in line with the brain's defense system.

With the *freeze response*, the child looks at you with a blank expression, like a deer in headlights, paralyzed with fear. In an attempt to stay safe, they shut down, unable to discuss the situation or process what happened. Younger children can neither understand your reasons for being angry nor offer an explanation for their behavior. Older children just shut down. It isn't an act, but an automatic response of the brain's emotional center.

Again, whether you are a child, a teen, or an adult, these behaviors are all fueled by the amygdala and cortisol. Too much cortisol in a child's system can erode healthy connections in the brain, leading to problems with concentration, memory, and self-regulation, making it challenging to access the parts of the brain in charge of thinking, learning, and behaving appropriately. While short occasional bursts of cortisol are expected and easily handled by the body, disease can occur when cortisol levels become too high due to daily stress.

When a child, teenager, or adult feels safe, the hormone serotonin is produced. Healthy levels of serotonin are necessary to make strong connections throughout the rest of the brain.

IMPLICATIONS FOR PARENTING

Every interaction we have with a child contributes to the development of pathways in the brain. I mentioned earlier that children are literal and don't understand intention. Rather, they interpret their experiences with concrete simplicity. When, in jest, we threaten to leave a young child with the monkeys at the zoo, they believe us. This is because the frontal lobes, the region of the brain associated with reasoning and solving problems, are among the last parts of the brain to mature.

If the brain is to develop to its maximum potential, a child must feel safe. When we are consistent in our expectations and responses, we contribute to a pattern of predictability that eventually becomes an automatic habit. By trusting we will never take our love away, the child's brain relaxes and the process evolves smoothly, uninterrupted by chemicals produced under stress.

How can we communicate safety and love to a child? The key is to stop what we are doing, get down to their level, look lovingly in their eyes, and speak calmly. If we are angry, we take responsibility and state that we feel angry. We model respectful behavior. When we breathe deeply and talk about our feelings instead of acting them out, we demonstrate how to deal with anger effectively.

Consider a situation in which a child's building blocks are scattered all over the living room long after we asked the child to pick them up. Instead of screaming, we can soothe our own frustration over the mess and say, in a gentle voice, "I'm angry that I asked you to put your blocks away and they are still scattered everywhere. Do you need help putting them away or do you want to do it by yourself?" Since children love to be playful, we can make cleaning up fun. We might challenge the child to see if they can put the red blocks in the appropriate container faster than we can do the same with the blue blocks. In this way the brain makes the connection that cleaning up can be enjoyable, that being loved feels safe, and that anger is an emotion that doesn't have to control us. If your emotions get the best of you, find a place to let them pass, engaging your child when you are feeling better.

While we live in the most advanced technological age in recorded history, the human brain continues to function as nature built it. A child's brain circuitry is wired to develop in a specific way and can't be rushed just because we live in a busy, stressful, technology-overloaded society. Even in the 21st century, a caterpillar needs to meticulously morph through the chrysalis stage before it becomes a butterfly.

Mother Nature doesn't take into account the complications of day care, divorce, blended families, or long commutes. Children continue to need adults who are present, aware, reflective, self-soothing, engaged, playful, consistent, and compassionate. Their young brains need to develop in an environment of safety, trust, and appropriate stimulation. Television will never serve as a substitute for human contact. Computers can never replace playful parental attention. Workbooks can't teach real-life experiences. Threats and punishments can never achieve what empathy and compassion can achieve. Lecturing children won't inspire them to reflect and grow. Sharing isn't something that happens on demand. The brain simply doesn't function this way.

It's imperative we learn how to set limits without the intrusion of fear. The reason parenting can be so challenging is that, without the use of threats and punishments, adults are left to do the hard work: get their own emotional and physical house in order and become educated in emotionally healthy parenting techniques.

The primary challenge as parents is to soothe our own anxiety. A parent who worries, weighs every decision over and over, projects into the future with angst, and emits fearful energy instills these negative traits in their child. Even when the parent smiles and uses soothing words, the child picks up on the adult's real energy. Because of this, my suggestion is to limit your own exposure to frightening news stories and conversations about sickness, disasters, and the horrors of our world. You may be surprised at how much negativity invades your thoughts and behavior in the course of a day.

A further challenge is to know how to create limits within a framework of trust and respect. Even the most educated parents miss critical elements that contribute to healthy emotional development.

In the quest for raising well-behaved, successful children, we often overlook the clues that let us know when our children are begging us to notice their cries for help. Misbehavior is always a signal that a child is struggling with something. Nothing can be more important than tuning into your child. Your responses are extremely influential in the way their brain creates habitual behavior.

THE IMPORTANCE OF STAYING POSITIVE

In a recent study, it was found that merely hearing the word "no" releases stress neurochemicals, reducing a child's functioning to that of the primitive brain.

When something feels like a threat, children lose the ability to think. They then shift into their fight, flight, or freeze mode. In this state, they forget the limits and can't make sense of our demands. It's therefore imperative to find a way to say "no" without actually using the word — with the exception of when they are in actual danger and we *want* the amygdala to spring into action. An example would be to insist they stop running in a parking lot because of the danger of moving cars. We want their memory of cautiousness to kick in whenever they are in such situations.

Young children can't process intellectual explanations and are concrete learners. If you don't want a toddler to touch something, the smart thing is to remove it from their reach. If you want them to learn something, the trick is to enter their world and playfully model the desired behavior.

Each moment of interaction is an opportunity to foster pathways in the brain that associate feelings of love or fear. I want to emphasize that you don't want to create pathways that tell the young brain that love and fear are emotional partners. You want a child's brain to connect loving to feeling safe, not to fear. As adults, we all need to remember what it felt like to be a child who was afraid of being alone, being punished, or being ridiculed.

Some experts believe it can require 2,000 or more repetitions for a child to "own" a concept. How much better to set up a loving learning environment than to control behavior using guilt. It's completely unnecessary and downright unwise to shame a child over what their brain isn't yet ready for.

Take sharing toys as an example. Instead of insisting a child share their toys, a wise parent provides safe opportunities for the child to experience sharing in a positive context. This can be done with a mature older child or adult in the form of games in an atmosphere of playfulness. Repeated experiences of feeling good while sharing become embedded in the brain, so that the child associates sharing with positive memories.

Despite all the research, some parents insist the use of fear is a good thing because it "works." Fear works well when it comes to getting us to buy products we don't need or to do things we don't have time for, but it's far from a healthy way to raise children. Parents who use fear may produce kids who acquiesce; but if they could see into their young ones' hearts, souls, and brains, they would notice a deterioration of the capacity to love fully, to embrace life richly, and to develop the cerebral cortex to its highest potential.

Children raised with fear tend to grow into adults who struggle with insecurity, self-doubt, perfectionism, a lack of trust, lying, and an inability to form healthy relationships. A child may appear successful on the surface but be an emotional mess on the inside. The fallout from being raised with fear is what keeps therapists and psychologists in business, not to mention making pharmaceutical companies wealthy from selling antidepressants and other mood-altering medications.

When it comes to influencing your child's brain, you are more powerful than you realize. You can fulfill the role of an active sculptor as the brain continues to be wired and networked through the first eighteen years of life — on this the scientific data is abundantly clear. The research is unanimous that children raised in nurturing environments learn compassionate connection. In contrast, when they are raised in homes lacking a strong parent-child connection, the neurons build pathways that develop reflexes for self-protection.

The human brain has the capacity to store all the memories associated with every experience we ever have. Our conscious mind may have lost touch with our memories of a disconnected parent, a humiliating event, a message of unworthiness, or a frightening experience, but it's all there in our subconscious. When something in the present triggers a sensation aligned with a memory, the amygdala goes into alert mode and we switch from being proactive to protective.

Raising children stirs up deep memories from our own growing years. If your child's behavior activates negative memories, you may find yourself reacting from wounds stored deep within your brain and be baffled by your actions. There's a way to identify and restructure the circuitry that causes us to overreact. We each have built-in radar that alerts us when it's time to pause, breathe, and rewire the pathways. Once we learn how to use this guidance system, we come into our power.

CHAPTER 8

HOW EMOTIONS FUEL BEHAVIOR

"Making the decision to have a child is momentous. It is to decide forever to have your heart go walking around outside your body."

— Elizabeth Stone

NOTICE YOUR TRIGGERS

Emotions are powerful. Sparked by thoughts, events, and perceptions, they fuel behavior. Understanding the relationship between thoughts, events, emotions, and behavior is imperative if we are to be empowered parents.

The people we most love have the ability to evoke our deepest emotions, which can crash over us like thunderous waves. Consequently, as ego is triggered by a child's behavior, we become reactive, which gives us a false sense of power, causing us to engage in the very behavior we promised ourselves we would never resort to with our children.

Internally, however, something quite different happens: we shrivel into powerless creatures. By reacting to our children's behavior as a result of our own emotions, we disconnect from our wisdom. This inevitably results in miscommunication, leading to needless power struggles — all because we have detached from our authentic power. Child and parent find themselves crying, screaming, threatening, nagging, or shutting down.

Adults who either detach from or overreact to their feelings tend to become parents who ignore their children's inner world. When discipline is influenced by the roller coaster of family emotions instead of being guided by best practices, everyone is negatively affected. Even with the best of intentions, parental declarations of love become tangled with guilt, shame, anger, and frustration when unresolved emotions are involved. For this reason, a wise parent is smart to ponder the role of their emotions in family dynamics.

WHAT'S THE EMOTION BEHIND THE BEHAVIOR?

The single most detrimental parenting error is to focus on changing a child's behavior without looking beneath the surface to see what emotions are causing both the child's behavior and our reactions. Many parents resist putting their emotions under the microscope because they don't want to know what's behind the masks they have created for themselves. They just want their kids' behavior to change! However, true parenting power is achieved by first addressing our *own* emotions as parents, since these drive our ineffective parenting techniques.

Children often become overwhelmed with emotion. At such times, it's vital to acknowledge what they are experiencing. Acknowledging emotions doesn't mean lowering standards or being inconsistent with limits. The challenge is to respond to the immediate situation by modeling the behavior we expect back from our children. Utilizing best practices means we encourage our children to express their perceptions. We then remind them that even extremely strong emotions are never an excuse for poor behavior.

As parents, when we are angry we tend to lash out with unkind words and explosive behavior. We use guilt, shame, threats, and sarcasm — yet we expect children to "be nice" when *they* experience frustration. If we want children to handle their anger without hurting others, it's imperative we are empathic when we are upset with them. The question to ask ourselves is whether we are getting in touch with the emotions fueling our child's behavior, or whether we are just demanding compliance.

Consider some of the scenarios in which we find ourselves triggered.

Your toddler has a meltdown when you take your cell phone away from her. As she throws herself on the floor, your frustration leads you to threaten, "Stop crying or you'll sit in timeout." Pretty soon you find yourself in a full-blown power struggle, wondering why this kid can't simply listen. You're screaming at your toddler to get their emotions under control, while you yourself are having an adult tantrum.

Here's your pivotal moment. As your child's protests grow louder, you soothe your own frustration and say, "I hear you. You wanted mommy's phone. You're angry, and I'm angry too." Staying close to the child with calm energy aided by deep breathing, you softly remind her, "We're going to feel better." The frustration will subside, and you will have the opportunity to open your arms and hug her as you say, "Whoa, we both feel better now, don't we." In this way, instead of demanding that she handle the same emotions that were difficult for you, you model soothing yourself, which encourages her to do the same. Just like in the red dress story, she learns that even when she doesn't get what she wants, she nevertheless feels understood and loved. Going forward, you make a mental note to keep your cell phone out of your toddler's reach.

Or take the case in which your four-year-old son tells you he hates the new baby. A flash of fear rips through you, so you tell him it isn't nice to say he hates his sister. Since he's afraid the baby has replaced him, insisting he's supposed to love the baby causes confusion and guilt, since he can't love the baby just because you demand he does so.

Here's your pivotal moment. Because you recognize your son is feeling confused, misunderstood, and unloved, the next time he's uncooperative or ornery, instead of demanding immediate compliance, you tend to his unspoken emotions by recognizing he's struggling with anger toward you for bringing home a baby who takes up all your time and has disrupted his world. You soothe your own stress and exhaustion, then sit down next to him and calmly say, "It's not always easy being a big brother. Sometimes you wish the baby would go away. How about we spend some special time together. What would you like to do with me?" By soothing yourself, you're able to acknowledge your son's inner world and meet his legitimate needs.

In yet another situation, your teen is crying hysterically because the boyfriend you never approved of is moving away. You reassure her it won't take too long to get over him and insist she's better off without him. She declares angrily, "You're the worst mother in the world. I hate you. I can't wait to move out of this house."

Feeling hurt and unappreciated, you scream back, "You're so ungrateful. I'm just trying to help you see that it's for your own good. Until you apologize, I don't want to talk to you." Such a reaction is counterproductive, since demanding an apology from children forces them to be inauthentic. Compassion for another person can't be awakened on demand, but must arise naturally. Children who are treated with dignity and respect apologize from an authentic desire not to hurt other people.

Here's your pivotal moment. Instead of taking your daughter's reaction personally, you understand that by having a boyfriend she felt secure. Something in the relationship was working for her. By rushing her through the grieving process, she misses the learning that comes from getting over heartbreak.

When parents don't recognize that their own inner tension is creating the urgency to rush through challenges, they rob their children of the opportunity to learn how to soothe themselves. The better approach is to tell your teen daughter, "This must be so hard for you. I remember what it feels like to have a broken heart. I'm here for you if you want to talk about it." In this way, even though her heart is still broken, she feels like you are the mom she would choose because you understand her pain.

Until we learn how to deal with our own emotional triggers, we are powerless to help our children deal effectively with theirs. Identifying what's swirling within us is the first step to moving out of reactionary behavior and into mindful solutions.

CHAPTER 9

HOW TO PARENT EFFECTIVELY DESPITE YOUR OWN CHILDHOOD WOUNDS

"Whenever we hear an opinion and believe it, we make an agreement, and it becomes part of our belief system."

— Miguel Ruiz

UNCOVERING YOUR WOUNDS

In an earlier chapter, we touched on how most parents are unaware of how their own early experiences influence their parenting. Now I want to go more deeply into how our own and our children's behavior are clues to what's happening beneath the surface.

A little boy in my preschool class lived with a mother who was extremely health conscious and insisted her child only eat the highest quality organic foods. His dad held a prestigious role in the community. They looked like a model family. I had to tell the parents their son was sneaking cookies out of the other children's lunch boxes. I was able to help his embarrassed parents understand that the way to handle this wasn't to punish him, but to give him something that looked as yummy as the other kids' snacks.

As parents, we can become so focused on what we believe to be our child's best interests that we lose sight of the larger picture and become slaves to an ideal. In this case, the mother relaxed a bit, found cookies made with healthy and natural ingredients, and was willing to meet her child's needs. The mother explained that because cancer ran in her family, she was afraid that if her children didn't eat healthily they would succumb to an early death. Layers of unconscious fears are often at the base of our masterful arguments for our parenting decisions.

In his book *The Five People You Meet In Heaven*, Mitch Albom states that all parents wound their children in some way — it's part of being human. We can lessen the damage if we are willing to examine our own inner world to identify what drives the way we relate to our children.

After a workshop in which I explained how our own early wounds can be triggered by our children's behavior, but we fool ourselves into thinking the huge reaction we are experiencing is because a request isn't being obeyed, a tearful mom asked to stay and speak with me. The evening before, she had lashed out at her ten-year-old son because he wouldn't take a shower. After he disregarded her many attempts to get him off the computer, she found herself screaming, "You're the child, and I'm the mother — I won't tolerate being ignored!" She described how her chest was tight with so much rage that it frightened her.

As we talked, it emerged that when this mother was eight years old, her ten-year-old brother began molesting her. Her son's refusal to listen to her unleashed the shame, fury, and sense of powerlessness that sprang from the tangled mess of her unresolved wound. Realizing the source of her reaction didn't mean she had to accept rude behavior or procrastination. But to not extend the chain of pain through the generations, she needed to do the work of soothing the trauma of her childhood. Some wounds are so deep that they beg for professional support. Even people with memories of a happy childhood carry within them unconscious anxieties and secret feelings of not being good enough.

By the time we become the head of the family, we are still learning how to express our own emotions in a healthy way. Consequently our tendency is to tell our children to stop feeling what they are feeling and just "behave well." When we do this, we prevent not only our children but also ourselves from getting in touch with the real issues.

I encourage parents to examine the messages they carry from their early years. Sarah grew up in a home in which she was given the message that she was responsible for the happiness of her family. If her behavior was off, her mother got a headache. She was told if she loved her mother she would do whatever was needed "so Mommy won't feel sick." She also received the unspoken message that the adults in the house couldn't handle her being in emotional pain, which meant she quickly learned to bury her feelings. When she married, she believed that if her husband loved her, he would do whatever she needed him to do for her to be happy. If he didn't comply, she took it as a sign he didn't love her. She was living with a "truth" from her childhood that was simply false.

There are many ways to resolve negative influences from childhood, and there's no right one for everyone. Based on our temperament and experiences, we each have to discover our own path to empowerment. A parent who realizes they are responsible for their own happiness gives their children the freedom to feel all of their feelings. But when parents consciously or unconsciously believe their happiness depends on their ability to control what their children are feeling, happiness is fleeting, since we can never effectively control another's feelings. Asking others to change their emotions so we can feel better always backfires.

GIVING UP WORRY

When we think disempowering thoughts, we experience disempowering emotions. These naturally trigger reactive behavior, since it's extremely difficult to respond to our children in a loving way when we are stuck in fear-based emotions. We cannot teach our children well-being from a place of our own fear.

When we question a thought instead of simply believing it because we've thought it for so long, or because others around us are sure it's true, we come from a place of authentic power. For instance, you might ask yourself, "Is it really true that if my child doesn't keep their room clean, they will grow up to be a slob?"

It's nearly impossible to make good parenting decisions when we are feeling worried, anxious, or stressed. Some actually wear these feelings like a badge of honor because they grew up equating worry with love. They approach parenting from the false belief that a good parent worries.

Many begin to worry about their children around the time they discover they are going to become parents. What has been referred to as the "mommy mind" syndrome begins with a flurry of information and a desire to protect our little ones from the dangers of the world. This intake of fear comes from the media, the internet, and conversations with friends and relatives. Add to this mix the messages we have heard since our own childhood, such as descriptions of a "good mother," stories of other people's tragedies, and warnings about the dangerous world in which we live. As children grow, the mommy mind provides fertile ground for thoughts that induce guilt and a compulsion to "do it perfectly." As one person caught in the mommy mind put it, "My thoughts are thinking me." She believed she was unable to tune out the daily cacophony of fear-based thoughts.

What she didn't realize is that this cycle can be interrupted. You can learn how to allow the negative energy to move through your body as you identify, articulate and acknowledge the truth of your feelings. The ability to come back into a state of balance, rather than getting lost and drowning in despair or fear comes from a willingness to shift your perception of the situation.

To stop the surge of worry in the heat of the moment is challenging. This is why many find it beneficial to create a daily routine of checking in with their deeper self and getting connected with the wisdom of their soul. The key is to find the practice that works best for you.

In my case, after years of saying, "I can't stop the flood of fearful emotions once they begin," I started to meditate. I found this process of focused breathing helped me quiet my mind, which cleared the way for inspired thoughts to float into my awareness. In this state of connecting to my inner wisdom, I received insights that assured me I didn't have to worry about my family's well-being. I came to trust that whatever challenges my children were facing were part of their soul's journey and for their highest good. Without these still moments, I would be left only with the fears and worries of my "mommy mind," easily forgetting that maturity, growth, and wisdom result from challenges. While it is easy to slip back into fear, worry or blame when new situations arise, it is especially important to remind ourselves that we do not have to get swallowed up by the details and that there is a stream of powerful guidance flowing to us at all times.

Whether you chose to quiet your mind with a walk in nature, a bubble bath, sitting in silence, snuggling with your pet, or asking for the help of a professional, going inward will offer you new insight. The answers to baffling questions may suddenly become clear.

Constant mind chatter and bombardment with things to fret about create an emotional tightrope parents walk on a daily basis. While it is natural for a parent to feel angst or concern periodically it is not healthy to be in a perpetual state of suffering caused by worrying about our children. We come into our authentic power when we are willing to pay attention to what's going on inside of us and take the actions that will shift our focus.

CHAPTER 10

WAYS WE TRY TO CONTROL
A CHILD'S FEELINGS

"The easiest thing to be in the world is you.
The most difficult thing to be is what other people want
you to be. Don't let them put you in that position."

— Leo Buscaglia

EMOTIONAL ENMESHMENT

There's a widespread belief among parents that as long as our children are experiencing strong negative emotions, we can't feel good ourselves. In contrast, when our children seem happy, we breathe a sigh of relief. "One less thing to worry about," we tell ourselves.

I have learned that we only step into our power when we no longer *need* a child to stop crying or start behaving a certain way so we can feel better. Children need to be able to feel their emotions without it tipping us off balance.

Many parents have a symbiotic relationship with their children, feeling emotionally immobilized until the kids feel better. Some even experience a physical stress reaction, feeling ill, depressed, or overcome with tension. In such cases we are overly connected to our children's emotions. When our own well-being is tied to a child's emotional state, we lose our effectiveness as parents.

The driving force behind the blurring of boundaries that occurs in families, whereby parents think they have a right to control their children, is what society generally refers to as a parent's natural love for their child. The problem is that this love is tinged with its underbelly, fear. As we saw earlier, fear often masquerades as concern and is the taproot of our need to control.

I recently worked with a couple who experienced opposite reactions when their son had a meltdown. The mother, who was sensitive and intense herself, became outwardly exasperated, coaxing and threatening at the same time. Deep inside she felt like a failure and wondered what went wrong with her dream of a happy family. She worried her child would grow up with chronic depression, just like her own mother. Having been raised with the belief that real men don't show emotion, the father made fun of the child and walked away at the first sign of distress. At such times the mother felt abandoned by her husband. Whenever he wanted to toughen up the child with physical punishment, she intervened to avert a spanking. Insisting it was her fault the child didn't listen, the father shut down, disconnecting from his family's emotional pain by turning his attention to work. Neither the mother nor father recognized the role their own early experiences played in the way they responded to their child.

While it's natural to feel anxious when our children experience negative emotions, it's important not to become so enmeshed with their struggles that we rescue them from their pain, demand they get over their emotions, or put up a wall that denies everyone's legitimate feelings.

It's normal for our own state of balance to be somewhat thrown off by our children's negative emotions; however, it's vital we learn to soothe ourselves. If we can't steady our own inner turmoil, we risk becoming an emotional controller.

When many otherwise reasonable and intelligent adults become parents, they find themselves emotionally unhinged. Consequently they miss the cues that they are becoming too enmeshed with their children. Such parents usually fool themselves by saying, "It's because I love my children that I do this. It's for their own good. Someday they will thank me." If you are an emotional controller, there's a greater possibility that someday they will be on antidepressants, engaged in some type of compulsive behavior, or seeking a therapist.

If we can hold our own emotions in check and allow our children to express what they are feeling, we create a stronger bond because they know they are totally accepted and safe. The reason most children don't confide in their parents is that past experience has taught them grownups can't handle the truth.

It will prove valuable to take a look at some of the forms in which our fear manifests itself. I identify nine fear-based ways in which we try to control our children's feelings.

THE FIXER

The fixer makes sure everything goes well so their child doesn't have to deal with frustration or disappointment. When the child finds something challenging, such parents can't bear their own discomfort. Examples of this are the mom who volunteers on the PTA to make sure her kid gets a part in the school play, and the dad who screams at the coach because his kid wasn't picked for the game.

The fixer is a slave to an unquenchable need to keep the kids happy, not realizing they are robbing their children of the opportunity to welcome disappointment and negative emotions as a natural part of their growing process.

THE LECTURER

The parent who responds to their child's questionable choices with intellectual explanations gets lost in a maze of analyzing and problem solving. However, a child who feels inadequate, ugly, not part of the crowd, stupid, frustrated, or fearful isn't motivated by facts. In some cases, when the child is in a raw emotional place, these intellectual explanations only amplify feeling bad about themselves.

THE NAG

The nag has a strong desire to teach their child to be responsible. Even though this parent has good intentions, they actually contribute to irresponsible behavior because the child starts to rely on their constant reminders instead of building their own good habits.

In the same way that the fixer and the lecturer can't bear their own inner tension when the child struggles, the nag has a hard time allowing the child to feel the consequences of their irresponsible behavior.

A secondary effect is that the parent becomes resentful when the child continues to need reminders.

THE GUILT TRIPPER

In an attempt to help children become more empathic, some parents are reduced to using guilt to talk their children out of their feelings. "How would you feel if they did that to you?" is one of the guilt tripper's favorite questions.

This approach doesn't teach children to care about others; it just induces guilt. When someone cuts you off in traffic and you react with anger, you aren't ready to think about what might be going on with the other person. Similarly, when a child is manipulated with guilt, they come to believe no one understands them. This does nothing to increase empathy, instead provoking a desire for revenge.

The best way to teach empathy is to talk about feelings throughout the day and wonder out loud how other people might be feeling. Patient skill building, rather than statements that induce guilt, is what turns the behavior around.

THE SHAMER

A parent declares, "You should be ashamed of yourself. You know better than that. How many time do I have to tell you?" Yes, they may know. We all know how we should act. But under stressful conditions, we often don't manage to behave as we should.

Perhaps a child doesn't have the skills to handle their emotions differently. They may know they aren't supposed to throw things, but when they get upset, they need help managing the anger that's taken over. Similarly, they may know they shouldn't run in the house, which doesn't mean they can make themselves walk.

"Knowing better" doesn't mean children can translate the intellectual understanding to their physical actions. There are many reasons they might act contrary to what they know they ought to do. It might mean they are testing boundaries. Or perhaps their young mind isn't able to anticipate outcomes in the way adults do. They need patient help expressing their anger appropriately.

THE SERGEANT

This parent runs the home like a military establishment. However, what might work for marine training or the police academy isn't appropriate for raising children. We are preparing children for life, not war — and they aren't our enemy.

When a parent relies on their rank to keep children in line, the home becomes a battle zone, with one side winning or losing. Instead of teaching children how to cope with feelings, get their needs met, and handle situations effectively, this approach teaches them to lie, cheat, and manipulate in order either to stay safe or get their needs met.

This parent says, "Shut up. Just stop it," "I'm the parent, that's why," "As long as you live in my house, you'll follow my rules," "Cut it out," "How many times do I have to tell you?" and, "March over to that timeout corner and think about what you did — and don't come out until you are ready to say you're sorry!"

While keeping our emotions under wrap or giving orders may be necessary in certain jobs, at home our role is to create a safe space.

THE BULLY

Currently there's much concern about bullying in schools and cyberspace. Unfortunately bullying is also happening in the privacy of our homes. Some parents demand their children "get over" their feelings because, as the parent, they can't handle them. This parent uses teasing, sarcasm, or threats of extreme punishment to shame the child into changing the way they feel.

The parental bully uses demeaning phrases such as:

- "Stop crying. It's nothing."
- "Big boys don't cry. Man up!"
- "Stop being so dramatic. Your face looks like a turtle."
- "You're nothing but a baby."
- "I don't care how you feel."
- "If you don't stop crying, I'll give you something to cry about."
- "Do it one more time, and I'll tell the policeman to take you to jail."

Research indicates that children who bully at school and on the internet have experienced bullying in their own family.

THE INTIMIDATOR

Some parents use their anger as a means of control, talking in a loud voice, making an ugly or scary face, using profanity, or threatening physical punishment. They take bullying to a stronger level.

Such parents use threatening phrases the likes of:

- "If you don't do that by the count of three, you'll get a smack on the head."
- "I'm getting the belt."
- "Do you want your mouth washed out with soap?"
- "Wait until your father gets home. He'll beat that smirk off your face."

It's painful to realize that in the guise of love, parents find themselves threatening their child's physical and emotional safety.

THE ABUSER

Parents who resort to physical abuse are coming from their own deep childhood wounds, coupled with distorted beliefs about discipline. Those who insist there's nothing wrong with pinching, spanking, or hitting are setting their children up for psychological trauma.

If you find yourself spanking, hitting, using a belt, or worse, it's a sign you are carrying trauma from your own childhood. The best gift you can give yourself and your children is to seek professional help. An emotionally healthy parent never needs to use physical punishment or extreme measures as a means of controlling a child's emotions or behavior.

Some parents see it as their parental right to use the methods research now decries. They don't realize this is a coercive use of power — the idea that "might makes right." Using such flawed approaches can never produce the trusting relationship you want with your child. There's a world of difference between fear-based compliance and an emotionally healthy child.

When love and physical pain are experienced concurrently during the growing years, children move into adulthood accepting the notion that someone who loves them has a right to hurt them. This opens them up to predators, since they think people have a right to touch them in ways that don't feel good. When a child says, "Stop, you're hurting me," a grownup must listen. Children have a right to have their body respected. Parents who are consistent in terms of limits don't need to resort to spanking or other forms of punishment.

Control under any guise, be it love, concern, or caring, is still control. It creates an illusion of a successful family. Power struggles, eating disorders, addictive behavior, and emotional shutdown are the result of caring parents succumbing to controlling techniques.

Once we learn to soothe ourselves, we can let go of our need to control.

CHAPTER 11

DEVELOP EMOTIONAL RESILIENCE

"I have come to the frightening conclusion that I am the decisive element. It is my personal approach that creates the climate. It is my daily mood that makes the weather. I possess tremendous power to make life miserable or joyous. I can be a tool of torture or an instrument of inspiration. I can humiliate or humor, hurt or heal. In all situations, it is my response that decides whether a crisis is escalated or de-escalated and a child is humanized or de-humanized. If we treat people as they are, we make them worse. If we treat people as they ought to be, we help them become what they are capable of becoming."

— Haim G. Ginott

EMOTIONAL HEALTH BEGINS
WITH MEETING NEEDS

As children grow, they inevitably encounter disappointment, sadness, adversity, and even at times trauma. To cope, they require sustained confidence, enthusiasm, determination, optimism, appreciation, and the ability to overcome adversity.

Teaching children to be emotionally resilient is among the most challenging aspects of parenting.

The key to building resilience is to make sure a child's essential needs are met when they are young. In this way they learn to approach any situation from a sense of adequacy instead of lack, a feeling of strength instead of weakness, and a mindset of capability rather than ineptitude.

As a child's fundamental needs are met, the child's confidence and sense of security increase. In other words, it's in the little things of everyday life that the strength to handle life's big challenges later is developed. As their needs are met, children gradually learn that they can meet their own needs when called upon to do so.

What are a child's true needs? Back in 1962, the psychologist Abraham Maslow defined "legitimate needs." His list, which is continually being updated, is part of the standard curriculum for teachers of young children. I believe it's also vital to impart this

DEVELOP EMOTIONAL RESILIENCE

information to parents.

According to Maslow's hierarchy, people have physiological, emotional, esteem, cognitive, aesthetic, spiritual and self-actualization needs. No wonder it is often challenging being a parent! We are so busy trying to get everyone's needs met that we frequently wind up exhausted and frustrated.

While it is reassuring to know that parents are not responsible for meeting every need their child has, it is vital to note that misbehavior occurs when critical needs are not met.

HOW TO MEET YOUR CHILD'S BODILY NEEDS

At first glance, a child's physiological needs seem easy to meet. In reality, in many homes they are the trigger for daily challenges and a cause of parental exhaustion.

Fresh air is essential for children and might seem an easy need to meet. Children need to run around outside as much as possible, engaging in old-fashioned fun. It's worth giving up some of their scheduled activities to make space for them to create their own forms of outdoor play.

Healthy food might seem obvious, though it's easy to fall into the trap of turning eating into a battle. As we saw earlier, one way to handle this is to take children shopping with you, making them part of the experience of selecting what they will eat. Children age three and over can have their own list, helping to choose the fruits and vegetables they enjoy. Practicality is important. For instance, be aware that if you bring home junk snacks, your children will beg for them. Also, it's wise to allow a picky eater to choose from a wide range of healthy foods. Equating food with love or using food as a guilt trip creates an unhealthy relationship between emotions and food.

The wise parent doesn't force a child to eat. Instead of making eating an issue of control, such a parent sees food as an opportunity for enjoyment and the expression of personal preferences. Engaging a child's help in shopping and cooking, playing "restaurant," and pointing out how muscles are growing strong are ways of bonding while making mealtimes pleasurable.

Creative food presentation is helpful. Kale chips, celery with peanut or almond butter, veggies dipped in dressing, smoothies, and soup are wonderful ways of offering healthy alternatives to junk snacks. Power struggles at mealtimes create tension that spills over into the rest of the day.

Sleep can be a challenge. Though we can't force a child to sleep, we can create consistent, relaxing rituals that foster a gradual transition into a drowsy state.

Even though we may wish we could simply put our feet up and relax with a glass of wine, we need to be ready to spend time moving through quiet evening routines with our children. A warm bubble bath, gentle massage, a story, and snuggle time are an invitation to dreamland. When these are done consistently, children learn to soothe themselves into a peaceful sleep state. This doesn't mean your toddler won't want to crawl into your bed in the middle of the night, but it does mean that with compassion and determination you can help your child feel safe and secure in their own bed.

Creating a sleep-inducing environment means shutting off the television and the computer an hour before bedtime rituals begin because the light from these technologies works against the production of melatonin, which induces sleep. Parents make a mistake when they yell at their kids to "get ready for bed" while the television is blasting or computer games are being played.

Children tend to sleep more restfully when they aren't overloaded with the evening news, violent television shows, or scary stories. Remember, your kids hear your conversations and feel your energy. The stress of everyone's day shows up in their dreams.

Sometimes it can be exhausting just meeting our children's physiological needs, yet they are crucial to a child's development and we are wise to make the necessary sacrifices.

THE IMPORTANCE OF PHYSICAL AND EMOTIONAL SAFETY

For a child to learn how to self-regulate, they must feel physically and emotionally safe.

In a fast paced, constantly changing family environment where adults are struggling to get their own needs met, it's no wonder children can't always fulfill their parents' demands. Parents are advised to take care of their own emotional life so they have something left to give their children.

When a crying baby is consistently responded to by a nurturing adult, their brain creates patterns of positive expectations. They learn their needs will be met, which allows them to move into the toddler years feeling safe. When children repeatedly experience balanced responses to even their most upsetting behavior, they learn to trust that life is good. This combined sense of safety and trust helps them tolerate their inner discomfort when a need isn't met immediately. In this way resilience develops. By discovering they have the ability to wait, the child increasingly realizes they can handle challenges without a meltdown. Through countless repeated experiences, they become the master of their discomfort.

So what do children need in order to feel a sense of physical and emotional safety?

First, only allow emotionally healthy caretakers to watch your children. Since friends or family members may offer to help, yet often resort to old-fashioned discipline techniques such as spanking or guilt tripping, this can be challenging.

Second, it's important to be your child's advocate, ensuring their environment is age and stage appropriate, as well as conducive to safe exploration. Be bold in declaring your intention to set up a home consistent with child development best practices. This includes giving lots of positive attention, spending time enjoying being with your child, non-judgmentally redirecting children when they forget what is or isn't okay, setting age-appropriate limits you and your partner consistently model, helping children through transitions instead of demanding immediate compliance, and never withdrawing your love or threatening to leave or give away a child because you don't approve of their behavior.

A chaotic or fearful environment hinders a child's development of the capacity to deal with the challenges of self-control, whereas a child who lives with consistency and a large measure of predictability learns how to soothe the emotional upheavals that are a natural part of growing up.

When I was director of a child development center, I observed a lot of parents handle the challenge of leaving at the end of the day. Stressed by their own busy schedules, many used fear to motivate their child, making statements such as, "If you don't leave now, you'll go into timeout when we get home," or, "Get going or there'll be no television tonight." Others exhausted themselves and their wallets by making extravagant promises in exchange for compliance, including, "Leave now and I'll buy you a toy at the store," or, "Be a good boy and we'll go to Disneyland for your birthday."

Then there were parents who used imagination, fun, and anticipation to get their child to leave, saying things like, "I can't wait to get home and play ball with you" or, "Would you like to jump over the cracks in the sidewalk with me?"

My favorite technique was used by the mother of an imaginative, creative little girl who was having a delightful time pretending to be a princess and didn't want to stop her reverie. The mother got down on one knee and whispered in her ear, "I'm going to hop out of the center like a frog. Want to hop with me?" She knew her child well! The little girl went after her and cried, "Wait for me, Mommy." Together they hopped out of the center.

FOSTER A SENSE OF BELONGING

One of the basic categories on Maslow's hierarchy has to do with belonging. All children share the legitimate desire to be seen, heard, and appreciated. They have the fundamental needs for attention, acceptance, affection, connection and inclusion.

While there is no one 'right' way to handle the typical

challenges that parents face I find that many conflicts originate from a sense of unworthiness. Unworthiness is a byproduct of unmet needs. If you do nothing more than recognize that inappropriate behavior is a cry for help, you are bound to see a transformation in your relationship with your kids. While it is most beneficial to begin from the time they are tiny, it is never too late to make a conscious shift in the way you interpret your child's actions.

All children need an abundance of positive attention. Driven by a strong desire to feel they belong and a need for reassurance that they are seen and heard, some kids will do just about anything for attention. A good practice is to show appreciation when you notice your child engaged in positive behavior. Rather than using the popular (but overused) shortcut, "Good boy!" or "Good job," which are actually judgments rather than acknowledgments, offer a short description of what you notice, such as, "Wow! You put all the trucks in the box. They look like the cars we saw in the garage." Sometimes all it takes is a smile, a wink, or a touch on the shoulder to let a child know you notice them.

With older children and teens, years of tension and power struggles often create a barrier for noticing the good stuff. It is the adult, not the child, who must take the lead in shifting the focus from what is going wrong to appreciating the little efforts of positivity.

And please, please, please, limit your time on electronic devices. It is hard to notice your children's delightfulness when your attention is focused on your cell phone or iPad!

It's important to know what to ignore, when to offer choices, and how to allow natural consequences to take their course. It's also vital to listen to ourselves, noticing how we contribute to the behavior we are trying to change.

Children also need to feel they belong to something larger than themselves and that they can make a worthwhile contribution. Parents serve as authentic role models when they include their kids in acts of kindness and compassion. I was recently inspired by a dad that I met while walking through the booths of a local photography exhibit:

I stopped to admire some photos and he started to tell me about his work. He said he had always loved taking pictures but when his elderly mom could no longer leave her home he began taking photos everywhere he went so he could share them with her.

As he described the joy his mother received from watching his videos his teenage daughter popped in to the booth. She listened as her dad talked about his passion for nature and for photography. He continued to tell me how his daughter often joins him as he currently takes photographs and videos to the local nursing home, sharing them with the Alzheimer's patients.

He started to choke up when he talked about the day the director asked him to stop taking photos of the residents. He thought that he had violated a policy but was reassured that the reason she asked him to put down his camera was because a patient who rarely uttered a word wanted to dance with him.

He reached out his hand and the elderly woman, who never showed signs of connecting with others, broke out in a giant smile as she melted into his arms. As he told the story, his daughter gave her dad a loving hug and I could sense a special bond shared between father and child.

Instead of lecturing her about the importance of being compassionate and kind, he included her in an activity that demonstrated respect and appreciation for others. Children who live with compassion tend to grow into adults who express compassion. Lectures do not teach. Children learn from what they experience.

BECOME A COACH FOR YOUR CHILDREN

Part of helping children become resilient is for the parent to become a catalyst for solutions. This involves learning to read a child's signals and deactivating reactivity before it has a chance to escalate. By encouraging conversations about positive solutions for challenging situations the parent can function as an emotional coach, inspiring their children to get their needs met in a healthy manner.

A parent who sees it as their job to correct behavior without acknowledging the cause or taking time to move through the underlying emotions unknowingly creates frustration, emotional wounds, and unnecessary struggle. Such a parent hasn't yet realized that a child's external behavior is only the tip of an emotional iceberg.

Whether a toddler won't share toys or a teen is hanging out with the wrong friends, our own sense of well-being is threatened when our child's behavior seems out of our control. We actually use the expression, "My child is out of control." What we mean is that we can't control their behavior, and we can't feel good until we get them back to a place where we regain our sense of equilibrium.

Take the case of four-year-old Jana. The challenge seemed to come out of nowhere. Mom was preparing dinner after a long day. Jana stopped playing and asked for a cookie. Mom responded,

"Not now. It's too close to dinner."

Even though Jana's mother kept her cool, the little girl started to whine. Trying to be patient, the mother explained the relationship between sugar, feeling good, being healthy, and saving an appetite for a yummy dinner.

Jana ignored the brilliant commentary, stomping her feet and insisting she was hungry and wanted a cookie. Since she's highly persistent, no explanation soothed her. Resisting the urge to threaten, mom again tried logic: "Why are you so upset? Didn't you already have enough junk food for one day? You know your tummy hurts when you have too much sugar. The dentist said too much sugar is also bad for your teeth. There's no reason to be so upset. Now stop whining and go play."

All Jana heard was, "Blah, blah, blah." When she continued to insist on a cookie, her mother felt she had lost control of the situation, experiencing a sense of complete powerlessness.

Whether the issue is getting children to eat healthy food, do their homework, put their toys away, stop fighting with a sibling, or quit hanging out with the wrong group, a parent becomes less and less empowered the more they attempt to control their child's emotions or behavior.

NEGATIVE EMOTIONS MEAN SOMETHING NEEDS TO CHANGE IN *US*

When we find ourselves in a situation similar to Jana's mom and start to feel a flood of negative emotions that naturally arise with parenting challenges, it's helpful to realize that such emotion is our guidance system reminding us that before we can be effective, something needs to first change in *us*.

As noted in an earlier chapter, once our emotional neurons fire, we lose the ability to use our frontal cortex, where our wisdom originates. This is how we can easily find ourselves yelling, threatening, or wanting to run away from home. Our primitive brain and our child's primitive brain are locked in a duel.

When this happens to you, there are several things you can do to regain your power, the first of which is to take a *parenting pause*. Take it right in front of your child if they are standing there with you. You are modeling behavior they can copy and that will serve them well. Breathe deeply as you take the pause, perhaps breathing several times until you are again on an even keel. By the time you have taken a handful of breaths, you might even feel like smiling.

As you breathe, name your own emotions out loud. Let your child hear you. Once again, you are modeling a healthy strategy for soothing yourself, thereby acting as a coach. Say out loud, "I'm feeling angry. I'm feeling frustrated. I'm feeling overwhelmed. I'm tired. I have to make dinner. I wish I could just sit and relax. I don't want to hear my child whining. I wish she would be happy playing." You might notice that as you say this out loud, your child stops whining and starts listening to you.

As you continue to breathe consciously allow the negative energy to move through your body without judging what you are feeling. This process allows the brain to prevent the amygdala from gathering more momentum, giving your frontal cortex a chance to take over so you can act from clarity rather than from raw emotion.

When things have settled, allow yourself to become aware of

your belief that you can only feel good if your child's behavior conforms to your expectations. Next, make a conscious decision to shift your thinking, thereby beginning to create new neural pathways. You might tell yourself, "I can feel good even though my daughter is upset. My equilibrium doesn't have to go out of whack because she is whining or argumentative. I can stay centered. I can use the parenting pause to name my feelings."

This awareness can now morph into the realization, "I'll be more effective in helping my daughter find her sense of well-being by staying calm. As I remind myself she's honestly struggling with something, I don't have to take this personally and I don't have to react in anger. I can help her understand what's happening inside her. I can regain my balance and stay committed to consistent limits. One of those limits is that cookies are out of bounds just before mealtimes."

Realizing we can stay connected to our wisdom enables us to relax as our brain releases the chemicals to open the pathways that allow us to return to our center. We experience a surge of clarity, which triggers compassion and our ability to find words of comfort to help our child begin a similar process inside themselves.

THERE'S LEGITIMACY IN THAT BEHAVIOR

A child's inability to articulate their needs is likely coming out in their whining and demanding. I suggest you don't tell yourself your child is just being manipulative. Research concurs that most of the time there's a legitimate need behind a child's annoying behavior. Young children can't always regulate their needs to fit grownup schedules, while older children crave a sympathetic, nonjudgmental ear.

Children who are more sensitive, intense reactors, or highly persistent have a harder time letting go of wanting what they perceive they must have once the thought takes hold. This is why I emphasize the need for consistent limits, so we don't find ourselves going through similar situations again and again. Consistency avoids having to talk a child out of the legitimacy of their desires, while we simultaneously acknowledge their feeling of disappointment.

A helpful tip is to begin statements with the word "yes" rather than "no." In the case of a child who demands a cookie, you might say, "Yes, I hear you. You wish you could have a cookie now. Hmm. Let's check and see if it's a cookie time. It's about an hour until dinner, so it's not a cookie time. Phooey. Since you are hungry, you can choose from the veggies in the refrigerator. Let's see what's hiding there. Oh, look, there are the carrots and cucumbers we bought when we went shopping together."

This is also a moment for reflection. Does your child need attention? Did she have a busy day in which she was asked to wait her turn, share her toys, and go in and out of stores? She might need five minutes of undivided time to unwind, or she may need to snuggle for a few minutes. Or you could say, "I'm thinking you might like to be with me while I get dinner ready. I could use some help picking out the peppers and tomatoes for the salad. We can sing songs while we work." If you run out of things for your child to do, have them set the table or reorganize your Tupperware drawer.

Certain behavior is predictable once a child reaches a particular stage. At each stage, clear limits must be presented in a way that makes sense to the child. A wise parent asks themselves this question: "Are the expectations and boundaries in our home appropriate for the developmental age of this child?"

Some four-year-olds declare their independence by *insisting* that mommy listen to them. If, by four, children haven't had sufficient opportunities to make their own choices and have a say in the way their day unfolds, they may become argumentative in an attempt to feel in control of their life. An empowered parent knows that children need a sense of autonomy within consistent and predictable limits.

Four-year-olds love to use their imagination as well as give inanimate objects human qualities. It's smart to play along with them. In the case of the cookie, you might say, "I wonder whether those cookies are lonely in the closet. Maybe they'll feel better if they know you can eat them after dinner. We'll tell them they have to wait a bit. We can wrap up two now and put your name on the napkin so they can wait for you on the counter. Would you like to do that?"

Later in the evening, as the child enjoys the cookies, you can talk about how good it feels to have figured out a way to make it all work. This becomes part of the process of learning to soothe themselves when they don't immediately get what they want. It's how resilience develops.

A modified version of this approach can be used right through the teen years. For instance, substitute cookie for using the family car. Parent and child do best when the conditions for saying "yes" to a request are clear and consistent ahead of time. When children are allowed to want something without the parent feeling pressure to either give in or try to talk the child out of the legitimacy of the desire, everyone is free to live out their dreams without holding someone else responsible for making it happen. We can respect our teen's wish to be independent and let them know that we trust they will figure out transportation issues when the family car is not available.

We help the situation when we willingly accept feelings of disappointment and offer alternatives if possible, refraining from a tone of judgment. If a teen has a meltdown, it helps to consider what might be going on beneath the surface and stay non-reactive. We neither cave in and hand over the car keys nor begin preaching about their need to be more responsible. Our willingness to soothe an urgency to teach lessons and instead, lovingly support our child in figuring out how to create the life they want, establishes a relationship of mutual trust and respect.

Whenever there's a sudden change in a child's behavior, it's worth considering whether larger factors may be involved. Are you getting ready for a move or the birth of a baby? Is there talk of sickness, divorce, or financial issues? Has the child recently seen a scary movie, played with older children, slept at a friend's house, or heard you arguing?

Children pick up on adult issues, on the conversations around them, and on television news shows. They intuitively know when concern is in the air. Their inability to make sense of it all can come out in whining, defiance, or sudden changes in behavior. Parents tend to forget that children are affected by holidays, family dynamics, changes at school, vacations, and fluctuations in schedules. Instead of simply demanding children behave well, find quiet time to wonder out loud with them and talk about the questions, insecurities or concerns they may be holding as situations at home and school move through the changing cycles.

In a workshop I was conducting, a young mother inquired what to do when a child has a meltdown in a public place. I asked her to tell the group what led up to the tantrum. She explained that she dropped her three-year-old at daycare at 7 AM and picked her up at 5 PM. They shopped in the supermarket for half an hour and were waiting in line when the child asked for a candy at the checkout. When the mother said, "No, we're going home to make dinner," the little girl began to kick her feet and whine. Aware of the judgmental faces around her, the mother felt she had to get control of the situation. But the more she tried to quell the fussing, the more intense it became.

Public meltdowns are often avoided when parents are attuned to their child's inability to handle exhaustion, frustration and marketing temptations. My first suggestion was to avoid taking a tired, hungry child into a store where candy is purposely positioned to invite desire.

When such excursions are unavoidable, the most a parent can do once the child is triggered is to remain calm and practice the following mantra, "What other people think is none of my business." This frees you to be present for your child.

Another suggestion is to jump into your child's world and rather than demanding immediate compliance, dream along with her. Remembering the red dress story, you can compassionately say, "You really want that candy. It's hard for you to see it and not take it home. The candy wishes it could go with you too, you both feel sad." Pack your groceries and make as quick an exit as you can, without indicating that the child is naughty for wanting something or withdrawing your love because her behavior embarrassed you. Allowing her to have her feelings and refocusing your conversation to the fun you will have preparing dinner together is part of the process of learning that life always works out for both of you.

I was recently out to lunch with some colleagues on what was a glorious day. We were at an upscale restaurant, sitting on a patio overlooking the beautiful San Diego Harbor. At the table next to us were a mom, dad, and child around the age of two. Mom and dad were engaged in adult conversation, with moments of acknowledging the child, who was playing with toys. After about fifteen minutes the child tried to get out of her seat. Dad cajoled her into "sitting nicely." Their food finally arrived. The little girl ate a bite or two, then again tried to get out of her seat. I heard the father say to the mother, "Do you think she has ADD?" I could hardly contain myself. ADD? This child was being asked to act like an adult! I had to control myself not to get up and take her out of her seat so she could move around as a toddler should.

ACKNOWLEDGE YOUR CHILD'S FEELINGS

Many children act out because they don't know what to do with their feelings, while watching parents model the opposite of what they expect from their kids.

Imagine coming home after a stressful day. You throw your keys on the counter, let out a big sigh, and your partner — who had their own stressful day — reacts to your grumpiness by asking, "What's up?"

You explain you had an awful day, during which your supervisor yelled at you, your friend gossiped about you, the traffic was impossibly slow, and you were pulled over for talking on your cell phone.

In that moment, do you want to be told you have nothing to be upset about? Do you want to be reminded that other people are struggling with much more challenging issues? Do you want it pointed out that you shouldn't have been talking on your cell phone while driving? On the contrary, you want soothing and a little understanding, not a lecture. You want to hear, "Wow, you had a tough day."

We all want to have our feelings acknowledged — something to remember when dealing with children, to whom feelings are big things. All of us need to be truly heard. When we are, we're more inclined to take responsibility for our actions.

We can help little children get in touch with their feelings by describing what we observe. We might say, "I think you are feeling angry. Something must not feel good right now. You wanted that toy. Mommy said you had to leave it. You are very angry. You are shaking your head and tightening your fists. I think you want to throw something. It is okay to feel angry, but it isn't okay to throw things."

As children grow older, we can encourage them to verbalize their feelings. Imagine your eight-year-old saying, "I'm angry. I hate my brother. He always teases me. I feel so furious when he does that. He's such an idiot." The key is not to react, thereby triggering guilt for his honest feelings, but to allow the child to express what he's experiencing.

At such a time, it's important to realize that the emotional explosion they are experiencing isn't necessarily what they are truly feeling. To understand the difference between an emotional reaction and our deepest feelings, think of a couple who have gone out for a romantic dinner on Valentine's Day and are anticipating a passionate time together later. However, on the way home they get into an argument. Instead of passion, they find themselves on opposite sides of the bed with a no man's land between them. The message from each to the other is, "Don't dare talk to me, let alone touch me." Though emotionally they have distanced each other, is the hostility they are manifesting what they are truly feeling? If you look closely, you'll realize they actually wish they could reach out to each other, though their ego won't let them. After a number of hours, or perhaps even a day or two, the emotional reactivity dissipates and they again honor their true feelings, which are feelings of connection. If they are honest, they wanted to be close all along, but their emotional reactivity buried their true feelings.

A child who is allowed to feel what they are feeling beneath their emotional reactivity may come to the conclusion, "I'm afraid my brother is right. Maybe I am stupid. Sometimes I feel so stupid, I want to hide. I get answers wrong in school and I'm embarrassed. The kids make fun of me." When the child can unearth the real feelings beneath the emotion, they will eventually learn how to resolve these feelings for themselves.

On the other hand, we cause the feelings to become deeply buried if, like so many parents, we say something to the effect of, "Don't talk that way. You probably did something to antagonize your brother. You're not always an angel yourself, you know. Now march into his room and say you are sorry for being so mean."

If a parent reacts by saying, "Just ignore your brother and he'll stop teasing you," or, "Stop whining," this child may never gain insight into their fears. Children who feel like this and can't express their truth often have stomachaches, headaches, and other physical ailments that parents try to correct with medicine. The medicine that's really needed is "magic heart medicine" — unconditional love that understands and accepts and is willing to have the tough conversations. By creating a safe place where family members are encouraged to uncover why they are reactive, parents become a channel for a child's self-discovery.

FORGET ABOUT "YES, BUT…"

If our intention is to create an emotionally safe environment, we have to stop twisting our interactions to get the kids to see things our way. This means becoming aware of when we say:

- "I understand, but…"
- "I hear you, but…"
- "I'm sorry you feel like that, but…"

The "but" in these statements is like a giant eraser, negating any intention of fostering communication. Whenever we say, "I understand, but," our children know that all we care about is changing their behavior.

The following scenarios illustrate how a parent can pivot to meet a child's needs and nurture the relationship by taking the "but" out of their statements.

When your two-year-old insists on carrying in a heavy bag of groceries, you might be tempted to say, "You want to help mommy, *but* the bag is too heavy." An empowered parent playfully says, "You like helping mommy. Here is a box of cereal for you to carry. Thank you so much." If you have a highly persistent child, you might keep a small grocery bag in the trunk that can be filled with light items so the child feels like they can do what mommy does.

You take your four-year-old out for the day, and he begs for a new toy. You might be tempted to say, "I hear you, *but* I don't have enough money." An empowered parent playfully says, "What a great truck. Should we tell it how much we wish we could take it home with us? 'Truck, we really want to play with you. We feel sad we can't take you home right now.'" If you have a highly sensitive or persistent child, they might need more reassurance that you understand the depth of their disappointment.

You find your eight-year-old watching television even though they are required to complete their homework first. You might be tempted to say angrily, "I know this is your favorite show, *but* your homework is still sitting on the table." An empowered parent waits for a commercial break and says, "This looks like a great show. Let's record it. I'd love to watch it with you after dinner." If you have a highly persistent child, they might need you to stay firm and loving as you record the show.

Your eleven-year-old sets the dinner table and makes place cards in honor of grandma's visit. Her excitement turns to dejection as she shows dad what she's done, and he says, "Looks nice, *but* why did you put my place card here? You know I sit at the head of the table." An empowered parent soothes his own emotions and says, "Wow, you put a lot of thought into this. You must be really excited about grandma's visit." A mature parent knows when to put their own needs aside to connect with their child.

Your teenager comes home, slams their bedroom door and refuses to come out. You may be tempted to say, "What's wrong with you? I know you're upset, *but* we don't slam doors in this house." An empowered parent gently knocks on the door and says, "I'm wondering whether you need time alone, or whether you'd like to talk about what's upsetting you. I'm here for you." The wise parent knows not to make the door slamming an issue in this moment, recognizing it as a sign of something big going on in their teen.

Many parents have become robotic in responding with, "I understand but…" When we deny a child's emotional world, rushing into defending our own position or desire to give advice, they learn to hide their truth from us. When you hear yourself saying, "I understand, but," or "Yes, but," stop and rewind and start again. Your willingness to do so has the potential to change your relationships with your kids... and everyone else as well.

You can practice saying, "I understand *and*" which can be followed with "I wonder, I'm thinking, I'm open to" as these words communicate your intention to really listen, to keep the dialogue going, to stay open-hearted and connected, as you invite an honest relationship of mutual respect and cooperation.

As you transform yourself from controller to coach, you can release your urge to manage what your child is experiencing by reminding yourself of the following best practices:

- You can expect cooperation as long as you consistently model desired behavior.
- You can learn to embrace your own needs and feelings without self-judgment or using unhealthy discipline techniques.
- You can hear the child's need for comfort beneath the tears and the whining.
- You don't have to talk your child out of their perspective or feelings in order to feel better yourself.
- You can take a cleansing breath and give yourself time to pause before you respond.

- You can let your children feel their emotions.

- You can love your children through whatever is occurring, without trying to rescue them from emotional pain.

- You can be tender and compassionate under all circumstances — to yourself, your partner if you have one, and your child.

- The most important outcome is that you stay emotionally connected to yourself and your child.

The more a parent gets in touch with their own emotions, the easier it becomes to validate and accept a child's inner world. When expressions of emotion no longer push our buttons, causing a sense of panic, we become free of the need to manage our children's feelings.

CHAPTER 12

HELP YOUR CHILDREN DISCOVER THEIR INNER GUIDANCE SYSTEM

"Your time is limited, so don't waste it living someone else's life. Don't be trapped by dogma—which is living with the results of other people's thinking. Don't let the noise of other's opinions drown out your own inner voice. And most important, have the courage to follow your heart and intuition. They somehow already know what you truly want to become. Everything else is secondary."

— Steve Jobs

SELF AWARENESS

In order for children to lead a life that authentically reflects their passion and purpose, it's important for them to become aware of and feel confident to follow their heart and intuition. However, it's difficult to encourage children to follow their inner guidance if we haven't experienced what it feels like to connect with our own. Parents who are willing to get in touch with their unconscious issues can become liberated from the illusion that good parenting is based on controlling their children. It takes a certain amount of courage to move past entrenched beliefs and start listening to the guidance that comes from our own inner voice.

One of the most empowering things I ever learned about emotions is that they are *a vital aspect of our inner guidance system* — a feedback loop intended to let us know whether we are moving toward or away from our deepest wisdom. When we feel optimistic, playful, and eager, we are in flow with life. Feeling good allows us to savor the deliciousness of a moment with our child. When we feel tense, fearful, or angry, it can be an indication from our consciousness that we are holding down repressed emotions or thinking thoughts that allow us to drift away from the wisdom that lives deep inside.

I used to feel an urgency to get rid of my negative feelings. The more I learn to embrace life exactly as it is, without trying to change anything or anyone, the more I realize that feelings are guidance and I no longer have to justify or banish the negative ones. I accept that they are merely indication that in that moment I have become disconnected from the Greater Wisdom that lives within me.

When I'm willing to take a breath, get still, and ask for guidance, I discover that I have access to seeing another side of my "story." It has been a messy process of learning how to release the egoic thoughts in my mind and start noticing the inspired promptings from a deeper place of authentic wisdom. I still get pulled down into doubt and negativity. Even the most conscious parent will feel overwhelmed, unappreciated, and out of control at times. What has changed is my ability to see negative emotions as a valuable reflection of something inside me crying out for attention.

As children, many of us weren't encouraged to connect with our inner voice. Perhaps we didn't even know we had one. Through conditioning, we were encouraged to listen to the voices of our family and of our society, and it's often the truth of others that continues to play in our mind. While much of what we were taught has been useful, it often disregards the existence of of our inward reality, causing confusion for us as we move into our parenting experience. When we become trapped in flawed thinking or buried emotions, we lose our inner compass and are often left wondering why we are triggered so easily, and then feel sad or guilty about the way we're handling things.

If we've had a busy day and begin yelling because toys are scattered all over the living room, it's possible that a thought like, "My child is a slob; I can't deal with the mess," is fueling the anger pumping through our body. It is also possible that at a deeper level we have thoughts that are so uncomfortable we would rather not look at them. For example, we may be questioning our job choice, fearful about our health, or annoyed with our mate. It is easier to just be upset with the children. If we find ourselves caught up in a pattern of feeling frustrated, yelling and blaming the kids for our out of control reactions, it's quite likely we are ignoring signals from our guidance system.

Acknowledging that negative emotions are caused by more than just our children's lack of responsibility allows us to stop trying to force changes in their behavior and begin looking for answers inside ourselves. Being open to another way of thinking about and responding to a messy room or unmade bed can be the first step in finding a more effective way of encouraging good habits. We might ask ourselves, "What would help me handle this challenge in a loving and effective way? Am I feeling overwhelmed by my busy schedule and passing the stress on to my child?" If we are stuck in our intellect, we might respond with this thought: "This is not about me. This is about the mess. Children should put their toys away." If we are unwilling to step back and allow new possibilities to emerge, we limit our ability to access a more creative and positive solution.

A willing parent can learn to move past their cognitive mind into deeper consciousness. You can reframe the way you interpret a challenge and look within yourself, asking why you are reacting with such intensity. It might be your temperament or a wound that's being triggered. As you begin this process of self-awareness, you probably won't be able to turn off your emotions in the heat of the moment, and it may help to take a shower, go for a run, or just take a few deep breaths. Once you release the urgency to get a task done and stop the flood of thoughts that drive your big reactions, you may find that the feelings begin to subside. Over time, you may notice that by becoming still, something else begins to surface — a prompting from a deeper place, the place where all of your wisdom and creative answers lie. You may be pleasantly surprised to discover that the answers to challenging situations suddenly become clear.

When we turn to well-meaning friends and relatives for advice about the best ways to "get" children to become successful adults, we often wind up following strategies based in fear and ego. Such tactics may coerce cooperation in the short run, but they usually rob both parent and child of exploring the authentic needs and emotions living beneath the surface of everyday life.

BLAMING OTHERS FOR OUR BEHAVIOR

A typical human flaw is to blame others for our behavior. When parents model this, they teach their children to do the same. It is vital that we catch ourselves when we start to rant and rave and actually believe that our children must change before we can regain our composure.

A person who comes from higher consciousness isn't someone who never feels upset, jealous, impatient, or angry. On the contrary, a conscious person experiences the full gamut of emotions. The difference is that we actually *experience* what we are feeling instead of acting it out. The vast majority of humans are quite unconscious of what they are really feeling. Many of us can emote, reacting with passion in our voice, face, or movements, but this isn't at all the same as feeling our feelings. To illustrate, imagine you have a romantic partner, close friend, or family member with whom you have planned a fun event, but an issue arises that causes you to become upset with each other. You get into a verbal exchange, following which you call the event off. The emotion that envelops you screams,

"Stay away from me — don't dare say a word!" If the person reaches out, you push them away.

Step back from your emotions just far enough that you can observe yourself in the grip of these emotions — and, in the example above, in the grip of the thoughts that triggered your outburst. From this more objective vantage, notice the emotion and its reactive character. Next, notice the feeling that's present *beneath* the emotion. This may be a little hard to do at first. But sit with the emotion until you experience a stillness inside yourself, at which point you'll begin to feel your true feelings. What you'll discover is a desire to connect. You may even find yourself wishing that whatever was said had never been said or that the thing that happened had never happened. This is because you have reconnected with your innate wisdom, your true self.

Let's look at a situation involving a stressed-out dad and his family. The stress is coming from immense pressure at work, since the project he has been dedicating all of his time, energy, and resources to is in trouble and he's on the verge of loosing the entire deal. If he does, the company will suffer a huge financial loss.

At the height of this overwhelming crisis, this dad arrives home to a chaotic household. Mom is yelling at the children to turn off the television and come to the table for dinner. When dad hears the children bickering, he says to himself, "I don't need this right now." As the bickering continues, the stress he's experiencing as a result of his worried thoughts concerning work causes him to lose it. As a feeling of rage sweeps over him, he suddenly slams his fist on the table, demanding the children either shut up and eat dinner or go to their rooms. Sitting in silence as he eats, dad emits strong vibrations akin to a powder keg that's ready to explode. The only emotion he's in touch with is his anger.

At this point many parents in such a situation might allow their anger to direct the rest of the evening. They feel entitled to stomp around, scream, swear, and threaten. After all, it's the children's behavior that's causing the tension in the house, isn't it?

Many adults lose their ability to navigate family life once they are stuck in their own inner turmoil. Unless they become attuned to the emotions swirling within them, and to the thoughts that may have triggered these emotions, then take personal responsibility, they are bound to fall into the typical parenting trap of believing that the only contributing factor to the chaos in the house is the children's lack of cooperation.

This dad would begin to come into his true power if he would get in touch with the frustration, fear, and sense of inadequacy he experiences at home and on the job — and especially with what he tells himself about the situation. To realize that anger is a reaction to his mental chatter about what he's been going through is the beginning of learning how to move into more effective ways of dealing with his challenges — and hence to being a positive role model for his children, who can learn from him how to deal with their own challenges.

LISTENING FOR INNER GUIDANCE

In order to be fully present with children, it's helpful to engage in some form of regular reflection and introspection. It's hard to get in touch with our inner guidance in a challenging moment if we don't practice mindful awareness during some part of our day.

There are many ways to connect with our inner wisdom. These include walks in nature, sitting in stillness, and reading books that offer processes for tapping into our deeper consciousness. Other approaches include guided meditation, prayer, and yoga. While there is no one right way, it's important to find what works for each of us and make a commitment to regular practice.

Connecting with our inner guidance often manifests in the following:

- We embrace life the way it is, instead of trying to change people and situations.

- We release the need to be right and become open to different perspectives.

- We see challenges as opportunities to grow and expand.

- We notice more aspects of our loved ones to appreciate and admire.

- We reduce time spent on electronic devices and stay focused in the present moment.

- We stop holding anyone else responsible for our happiness.

- We sense our well-being even in the midst of chaos.

- We release anger, resentment, envy, gossip, or feeling like a victim.

- We notice how patterns in our life keep reappearing, constantly offering us a mirror into our soul.

- We embrace the wide range of human emotions as part of a messy process that's necessary for living a life that's fully alive.

- Answers to challenges that used to baffle us suddenly become clear.

ENCOURAGING CHILDREN TO
USE THEIR OWN GPS

We are all born with an active internal guidance system. Sadly, many parents talk children out of what their guidance system is telling them. In contrast, effective parenting gives language to this guidance. The same way we teach children to brush their teeth, eat healthily, and get sufficient rest, we can encourage them to embrace their inherent wisdom.

Inner guidance shows itself early. For instance, anxiety around strangers is sensed between six and fifteen months, as babies begin to identify with their primary caregivers and no longer feel good being handed off to someone unfamiliar. They don't understand that grandma's feelings will be hurt by their refusal to melt into her arms. Neither do they realize the new babysitter is a really nice person, or that mom and dad desperately need an evening to themselves. The whimpering, clinging, and full-blown sobs are a baby's expression of their inner guidance.

If we don't recognize that a youngster's feelings are their means of guidance, we will tend to coax the child to ignore their intuition. A few years later, after we have successfully shamed the child out of listening to their GPS, we decide it's time to teach them to be afraid of strangers.

I have heard parents instill fear in their kids by saying, "Never talk to a stranger. A stranger could steal you away and you'd never see mommy or daddy again." My heart aches when I sense the terror in the parent's voice and the fear and confusion in the child's eyes. Remember, children take things literally. Consequently, the child wonders who exactly a "stranger" is. Should they say hello to mommy's new friend? Is it okay to talk to the mail person they wave to every day? Can they allow their eyes to meet those of the person at the grocery checkout? The child already had a built-in sense of who *felt* safe and who didn't, which they can no longer access because we talked them out of it.

When our child's GPS doesn't guide them into pleasing us, we are likely to end up resorting to scary stories and a system of confusing rules. However, we create havoc when we talk our children out of their natural instincts and replace them with guilt or fear. It's so much healthier to support our young people in trusting their God-given instincts.

By encouraging your child to connect with their deeper awareness, you will be nurturing their ability to check in with themselves when faced with the inevitable challenges that are part of the growing years. When friends put pressure on them to engage in behavior that's unsafe or unwise, tuning into their inner wisdom will become the guide that steers them to make responsible decisions.

WE TEACH WHAT WE LIVE

Once we experience the power of connecting to our inner voice, we recognize how important it is for our children to be able to access this voice in themselves. An effective way of helping them find their inner voice is to acknowledge their feelings and not try to talk them out of them. Saying things like, "Forget it, ignore it, no biggie, it doesn't matter, just be quiet and don't think about it anymore," teaches kids to stuff their feelings away. The more self-awareness we develop, the more we become able to help our children develop self-awareness. The more we become able to navigate the vast range of human emotions in ourselves, the more we become role models and the greater the likelihood that our children will be able to navigate their emotions effectively.

Imagine that you have a constant struggle to get your child to complete his homework. It may be tempting to make the judgment that your child is lazy or perhaps worry that he has ADD. The thought may occur to you that if he doesn't do his assigned half hour of reading every day, he won't progress to the next grade. If you can detach from the terror that has been triggered in your heart by the image of him not getting into a prestigious college, you just might get in touch with deeper realizations that can set you and your child free.

You might ask yourself, "What is it about this situation that triggers me?" Perhaps you realize that you feel like a terrible parent when the teacher sends home a note saying your child's homework is incomplete. You might notice your own childhood need to please people in authority is being played out through your child's school experience. Your ego might be kicking up a fuss as you realize how embarrassed you will be when you tell your friends that your child's academic achievement is below expectations.

You can choose to see the homework challenge as an opportunity for you to practice accessing your own inner wisdom. The next time your child procrastinates, you can ask yourself how you are feeling in the moment. What might you need in order to be patient and present for him? You don't have to have all the answers. You can even feel frustrated. Becoming aware isn't about becoming a perfect parent. It just means you are willing to go deeper and look at the real source of your discomfort.

Homework issues can be an opportunity to encourage your child's self-awareness. My experience indicates that children who refuse to complete their assignments have more going on than just being noncompliant. They often feel "dumb" or believe they are incapable of doing a good job. Some don't have the ability to sit still or focus for more than a few minutes at a time. Others need to feel a sense of their own empowerment, and after a long day of being told what to do rebel at the thought of having to do more work they don't enjoy. Once you clear away your grownup emotional baggage, you can help your child get in touch with his own truths.

One way of helping the child connect with inner guidance is to suggest that he ask himself what it is about the homework that feels so unpleasant. Does he need time to chill out or do something fun with you before settling down? Might he be feeling over-controlled, so that homework protests have become a form of feeling empowered? At first he may not uncover any great clarifying insights other than "it's boring" or, "I don't know." If you can stay centered and not get triggered, you might then ask the child what he needs in order to get his assignments done. While there's no instant magic, it's important to stay present with your child and allow him to find his own way of comfortably moving through the task. By staying non-reactive, you avoid becoming enmeshed in typical power struggles. Your ability to soothe yourself, remembering what a glorious being your child truly is, gives you space to allow inspired thoughts to come through.

While it may take many days of practicing this patient approach before you begin to see a shift in your child's performance, the relationship credit is deposited immediately.

A GIFT TO OUR CHILDREN

When we do our own inner work, we become more skilled at shifting out of reactivity. Our willingness to practice a more conscious parenting approach gives our children a priceless gift. Instead of being trapped by a flash of anger or a tightening in our belly, causing us to push our child away, we learn how to breathe through the urgency and allow it to settle down. In this way the energy of the situation can become useful rather than destructive.

Patrick, daddy of Rose and James, started attending my parenting classes to learn how to cope with his delightfully strong-willed children. Being a sky diving instructor, Pat had the type of schedule that allowed him the flexibility to be home with his family many afternoons. On the day of this story, he was in charge of the kids while mom did some errands. With almost two years of parenting workshops completed, he was pretty confident in his parenting skills. But when he left the children playing quietly for just a few minutes, he returned to what he described as "a disaster." In the short time he was absent, a mystery person climbed up on the counter, opened the cabinet that housed the baking supplies, and spilled flour all over the kitchen. His initial reaction was to gasp, feel his pulse quicken, and sense his muscles spasm. He began screaming at the children, demanding to know who was responsible for the mess. Rose blamed her little brother, whereas James insisted it was Rose's idea to make cookie dough. Pat felt himself totally out of control as he tried to clean the powdery mess from the children's hair, the grout on the counter, and the tile on the floor. He sent the children to their rooms, demanding that they stay there until they told him the truth.

This is my memory of what he said happened next: "It was as

if a light went on inside my heart. Right in the middle of my tirade, I was suddenly filled with the awareness that I didn't want to be this angry, screaming daddy. Something welled up from deep within me, and I softened. I no longer felt a need to yell." After a moment of regaining his balance, he walked into Rose's room and, with a tone of compassion in his voice, invited her to sit with him. At first she was tentative, as if her inner guidance held her back from trusting what would happen next. He tenderly looked into his daughter's eyes and apologized for scaring her with his big, angry reaction. He acknowledged how important it was for them to be a team and to trust each other. He said he would try not to act so scary when he felt angry. They hugged, and Rose admitted she took the flour out of the cabinet so they could bake cookies together. They agreed that, going forward, the upper cabinets were reserved for the grownups. Then she happily skipped off to James' room to play. A few minutes later Rose returned and said to Patrick, "Daddy, remember how you said we would always tell each other the truth? Well, I have something I need to tell you." Patrick held his breath, wondering what secret she was about to reveal. "Do you remember when we left cookies for Santa Claus last Christmas Eve?" she asked. "Well, in the middle of the night, I snuck into the living room and ate two of Santa's cookies." She waited to see how Patrick was going to react, perhaps checking to see if he would get angry. Instead of becoming angry, he hugged her and said, "I feel so good that you felt safe to tell me that story. I think that Santa has forgiven you, too."

The miracle of this story is the way the "disaster" led to the development of trust between father and child. Beyond taking parenting classes, Patrick was committed to his own inner growth. He had begun reading books about mindfulness and spent time each week in quiet meditation. His desire to live in full awareness and take responsibility for his reactions expressed itself as a priceless gift of trust for his child.

We encourage children to tap into their Inner Wisdom by being open and unafraid of having deep conversations. Some people refer to this guidance as coming from God, the Universe, religious practice, angels, guides or departed loved ones. Allowing children to wonder out loud about their Inner Being can spark a delightful discussion at the dinner table, in the car or at bedtime. This is not about dogma or about guilt. It is about getting still and discovering a sacred relationship with our deepest self. Don't be afraid to talk about this stuff with your kids. If you remain open to growing in this area, your children will be more than willing to talk about their Inner Being with you.

CHAPTER 13

TAP INTO YOUR PARENTING POWER

"When I look up at the night sky, and I know that, yes, we are part of this universe; we are in this universe, but perhaps more important than both of those facts, is that the universe is in us."

— Neil deGrasse Tyson

EVERYTHING IS ENERGY

Said Astrophysicist Neil deGrasse Tyson, "Many people feel small because they're small and the universe is big, but I feel big because my atoms came from those stars. There's a level of connectivity." *Connectivity is at the heart of authentic parenting.*

Energy operates in our lives whether we understand it or not. To help leverage our parenting power, I want to go a little deeper into how the energy of our thoughts, feelings, emotions, and actions affects others. Once we understand energy alignment, our approach to parenting changes. We find we don't have to control by nagging, yelling, punishing, or rewarding, since with alignment comes true power.

Without even being aware of it, we interact with energy every moment of our lives. When we turn on the television or car radio, or use the internet or a cell phone, we are accessing energy. Though the capacity to communicate through cell phones and the internet always existed, only recently have we learned how to harness this power.

When riding in the car, if we want to listen to music, we must tune our dial to the precise wavelength on which a station transmits the kind of music we enjoy. If our dial is slightly off, we get annoying static instead of a clear connection. If our phone carrier doesn't have sufficient cell towers, we experience the frustration of a crackly or dropped phone call.

Whenever we interact, we transmit not only information but also feelings, moods, and subtle cues. If we aren't aligned with our own center, the love and joy that naturally flow through us are hampered by the static of negative thoughts and reactive emotions. Consequently our communication is often interrupted by dropped signals. As humans, our personal interactions are energetic. If we want harmony in our family, the way forward is to embrace the energetic aspects of relationships.

Few parents realize the same expansive forces that formed the universe, gave us our DNA, and run our modern technology can attract cooperative behavior from children — and equally trigger reactive behavior. Just as writing on clay tablets evolved into writing on papyrus and eventually paper, and writing by hand led to typewriters, which in turn morphed into computer keyboards and touch screens, so too the various approaches to discipline advocated for centuries, even thousands of years, are today being superseded. Understanding that energy governs our connection to each other enables us to let go of old-fashioned discipline techniques. We move into a 21st century understanding of parenting power that truly works miracles.

THE IMPORTANCE OF SURRENDERING
TO ENERGY

In the same way that gravity is a force, our thoughts and emotions act as a magnet between our nonphysical inner world and what we experience in our external world. The thoughts we think and emotions we feel form an energetic pathway for this energy. Once we realize this, we understand that parenting isn't fundamentally about disciplinary techniques, as so many mistakenly imagine, but about harnessing our attractive energy.

I mentioned in an earlier chapter that when we think thoughts that bring on feelings of annoyance or powerlessness, the mind offers up more thoughts that are energetic matches to the feeling of annoyance and powerlessness. If we have what we perceive as a negative experience, followed by another, we can begin to feel stressed, exhausted, and perhaps victimized. Our thoughts may carry us back to when we had similar experiences in the past, or we may start projecting a future of such experiences. We create a "perfect storm" inside our head. The more the storm builds, the more likely we are to turn it into a self-fulfilling prophecy.

When we focus on the things our mate or children are doing that cause us annoyance or worry, it doesn't matter how right we are because our attention to the unwanted will only create more of the same. But equally, positive thoughts, perceptions, and feelings attract more of the same. It's therefore to our benefit to make a conscious decision to focus on behavior that pleases us, feels good, and that we want more of. By so doing, we take control of the only thing we ever have control over — our own response to life.

While words and actions are powerful, the definitive force in relationships is unseen energy. We are often unaware of the impact energy has on our children's behavior. For instance, you tell your child, "It's time for bed." While you read them a book you are secretly wishing you were free to go out with friends because you feel trapped in your parenting role and wish you had more freedom. Even though you are going through the motions of reading the story, your child can feel your disconnection. Their behavior will be a perfect reflection of your energy and instead of soothing into sleep they may cry, insist that you stay close or wake up and climb into your bed. You may become frustrated and angry because the child is not giving you the free time you desire. Once you understand the way energy works you can observe how your thoughts and your child's behavior are a perfect energetic match. Behavior that indicates disconnection or lack of freedom may flood your experiences with this child.

The way to turn it around is to acknowledge your legitimate need for time to yourself. Making plans for grown up time may immediately release some of your negative energy and allow you to authentically enjoy being with your child. With that said, I feel compelled to remind parents that children are not responsible for the adult's happiness and we must always be sure to make decisions based in best practices.

I suggest that you watch the way children behave with different people. The very child who whines and is demanding with a parent can be a sweet, delicious and cooperative 'angel' with another person. In many cases there is 'energy alignment' of conflict and struggle in one relationship and 'energy alignment' of ease and flow in the next relationship. Parents often interpret this difference in behavior as manipulative. It is actually a natural result of vibrational attraction.

Thoughts that we allow to consistently live in our head take on more and more power and eventually become manifestations as our children and others mirror back to us through their behavior. The key to working with the energetic laws of the Universe is to soften the urge to fix or control our children, other people or situations. When we give up our resistance to what 'is' and what must be different before we can feel good, we begin working with, rather than against, the natural flow of energy.

A passing thought does not create a pattern but continual thoughts in a negative or positive direction create a momentum that eventually become reality. When we pay attention to our feelings and the thoughts that trigger them we can learn to shift our attention and harness an attraction power that can bring us closer to our dreams. Parents who live in this awareness can share the on-going process with their children and become a model for attracting positive experiences into their lives.

HOW TO ATTRACT WHAT YOU WANT

The more in touch you are with the intuitive messages from your Inner Being, the easier it becomes to replace fearful thinking with sparks of confidence that come from a deeper knowing. Notice when discouragement, uncertainty or insecurity creeps into your mind. In the middle of complaining, gossiping or worrying, you can lovingly remind yourself that you can refocus your stream of thought. When stuck in negative thinking, the reason you feel so bad is you are receiving a signal from inner guidance that you are on the wrong track. It doesn't matter if the facts appear to create a compelling reason to jump into fear based behavior. The way to attract what you want into your life is to stay in touch with your spiritual center, the place from which authentic wisdom and joyful living emanate. Reaching for thoughts that take you back into your natural alignment can literally change the cellular structure of your body.

Because of the way energy works, if we are worrying about our children when we say we love them, what they attract from us is fear, not love. For example, when we serve organic fruits and vegetables but constantly dwell on sickness, emphasizing such things as "cancer runs in the family," we undo much of the good we accomplish with healthy food. When our teenager takes the car and we are constantly feeding them statistics about car crashes, we attract a vibration that matches disasters. We help our kids attract more wellness into their lives by reminding them, through our messages and modeling, that everything is possible, it is good to dream, we deserve to be happy, the present moment is where all our power is, appreciation is the key to joy, every choice we make affects our future experience, and life is supposed to be full of constructive fun. When we teach that, through our own behavior, lectures about health and safety become unnecessary.

The laws of the Universe never operate with the intention of punishment. Energy alignment is not about being good or bad. The challenge we face as humans is a learned tendency to notice something in our physical world and then get triggered into a web of thoughts, emotions and reactions. We quickly disconnect from our essence as other people's behavior controls our responses. We harness the magic of energetic law by observing ourselves, getting still, breathing slowly and deeply, allowing the flurry of thoughts and feelings to pass, breaking through old barriers and being open to the truth that lives outside our present comfort zone.

We give our children a priceless gift when we model this attractive power in our lives. While no one does this work perfectly, those who are committed to inner growth by taking responsibility for their own happiness cannot help but radiate with the energetic current of authentic love.

A DAILY TUNE-UP

In the same way a musician spends time aligning their instrument to vibrate in musical harmony, it can be helpful for many parents to give themselves a daily tune-up so they are prepared to respond to their children from a frequency of well-being.

When it comes to how to conduct a personal daily tune-up, I would like to share with you some suggestions that have worked for thousands of people and may work for you:

- If it feels good to you, before getting out of bed in the morning, treat yourself to a few minutes of "snuggling with God." Bask in feeling protected, loved, and guided. Rather than allowing your mind to take you to the concerns and fears of the day, take charge of your thoughts and make a mental list of things that are working well in your life. See your children thriving through their day. Remind yourself that happiness exists in this moment, not when the people in your life finally behave according to your expectations.

- Give yourself a few minutes of alone time before you interact with the children. Some parents purposely set their alarm early so they have time to do a quick exercise routine or short meditation. When you go into the bathroom, take a cleansing breath and look into your eyes in the mirror. Talk to your soul. Remind yourself you are worthy and loved where it really counts, between you and your spirit. Trust your inner wisdom to guide you as you move through your day.

- Remind yourself that being "right" is never helpful if it takes you to a place that feels bad. If you can't find specific things to feel good about, turn your attention to the sun, the moon, the stars, the trees, the warmth of your bed, your child's eyelashes — anything that aligns you with positive energy.

- Throughout the day, allow your awareness to drift to good times: giggles, hugs, high fives, snuggles, kisses. If you feel remorse or longing, it's time to get back to more general thoughts.

- Remember that all humans need to feel acceptance, appreciation, affection, approval and receiving of positive attention. Take time to nurture yourself so you have a generous amount of loving energy to share with your family.

- Become aware of your thoughts and emotions at bedtime. Make a mental or written list of everything that went well in your day, that's beautiful in your life, that you appreciate, or that just feels good. This might mean giving up old stories, old hurts, and fears for the future. Everyone has a different way of making this work for them. I've stopped watching the late night news and instead read from an inspirational book just before drifting off to sleep.

Parents want to know how to handle daily challenges. There isn't a single answer that applies to every situation. Within each of you is a stream of wisdom... and a daily tune-up can help you tap into it.

As your child notices the difference in you when you are in tune with your Inner Being, you'll naturally serve as an inspiration

for them to live from their highest self. This is parenting at its best —
parenting from a place of authentic power.

CONCLUSION

"You don't have a soul.
You are a Soul.
You have a body."

— C S Lewis

OUR SOUL'S JOURNEY

As we raise our children, we can easily forget we are being trusted to nourish not only their body and mind, but also the deeper aspects of their soul.

The relationship between body and soul is a private affair. No other human being can ever truly understand the intricate details of this personal connection. The most loving and caring parent can never fully comprehend the journey of their children's souls. Each of us must figure the journey out for ourselves. An empowered parent works on their own soul's state, while encouraging their children to nurture their private dialogue with their inner wisdom.

Children growing up in the same family and from the same parents experience different challenges. This is because each child comes with their own spiritual intentions for expanding and evolving. As we expand our own awareness, we realize we can have a huge influence on our children, but ultimately their journey is theirs alone. An empowered parent nurtures their own spiritual life without forcing their children to do so in the same way.

Children hate hypocrisy. If you give lip service to a spiritual life, yet in everyday reality are angry, resentful, afraid, judgmental, or unwilling to talk about your own limitations, your children are likely to reject your framework of spirituality.

PASSION AND PURPOSE

The more we connect with the wisdom of our own soul, the clearer it becomes that our children aren't our possessions. We understand that we are intricately related and have a special place in each other's lives, but our children's reason for being isn't to meet our needs.

Our children don't come into life to please us, emulate us, or make us proud and happy. They are here to figure out who they are, to understand the purpose of their gifts and challenges, and to have their own unique and personal dialogue with Ultimate Reality. Their purpose is to fulfill the blueprint for their soul's journey. Their life belongs to them. The wise parent lives their own life well and encourages their children to do the same.

As parents, we can feel the thrill of our children's growth and find pleasure in their achievements. But once a parent measures their own worth through their child's accomplishments, they become enmeshed. This all happens so unconsciously that we may not even be aware we are enmeshed. The trap is set the moment we become a parent.

Each day, it's important to remind ourselves that our children ultimately belong to no one but themselves. Living deep within each child is the seed of their destiny. Our role is to provide a rich environment in which the seed can flourish. Our encouragement of them to discover their essential nature is a crucial aspect of effective parenting.

In this vein, it's important to check in with ourselves to see what messages we are giving our children. Listen to the way you talk about them, since language is a clue to how we see our children.

Consider some of the things parents often say:

- "He's my little man."
- "She's my little princess."
- "He is going to play professional football"
- "She is our future doctor."
- "Everyone in our family plays the violin."
- "There's a right way and a wrong way, and my way is the right way."
- "I know what's best for you."
- "You are going to college whether you want to or not."

You can help your child get in touch with their own soul by changing the kind of statements you make, such as:

- "It was fun being with you. I can't wait to do it again."
- "You had such a big smile on your face, I bet you enjoyed that."
- "You must feel good about yourself. Even though that was challenging, you did it."
- "How do you want to do it? You choose."
- "Why don't you decide? You can always try it again if you change your mind."
- "You'll figure it out. You'll know what feels right for you."
- "Everyone gets to do it their own way. Your way may be different from mine or anyone else's."

Some parents think of religion, customs, rituals, and family traditions as soul activities. While these work for some family members, many children need to discover a different formula for being true to their soul. It's a cause of much tension and turmoil when adults demand children follow a prescribed pathway. Fear, guilt, shame, and coercion are never productive conduits for experiencing the loving energy of authentic being.

GIVE UP CONTROL

"Beautiful Energy, Source of my child's creation, You trusted me to be the parent of this unique and wondrous being, please guide me; fill my mind and my heart with inspiration so that I may be the parent this child needs me to be."

This is a prayer I was inspired to repeat over and over when my children were little. Each time I consulted my Inner Being, I received the same message: my role as Matt and Melissa's mother was to love them exactly as they came to earth. They were perfect and didn't need me to change them. I had to give up my preconceived ideas about the way children needed to be, along with my concern about what others thought. The more connected I was to my own center, the freer I found myself to adore them, appreciating their ability to march to the beat of their own drums.

Our challenge is to let go of needing to be the source of our children's well-being. We are merely the conduit through which our children are brought into life. They come into the world riding the currents of the universe. When we try to impose a previous generation's set of rules or standards on a new wave of humanity, we push against the current of societal evolution. But if we acknowledge a child's soul as the captain of their ship, we release them back to their authentic purpose for coming here.

When we get caught up in our own agenda, we miss the

wonder of our child's uniqueness and suffer the stress of trying to mold them into the vision of our own desires and expectations. Empowered parents understand that infinite intelligence flows through all children, and we have the ability to encourage or diminish that flow.

Every moment with your child presents an opportunity to either connect or build walls. Connecting with your child is like making deposits in a joint emotional bank account. The more moments spent building trust, confidence, and appreciation, the more you have to fall back on when times get tough.

Banking a strong connection with a child so that we weather difficult times occurs in the ordinary events of everyday life. For example, twelve-year-old Angela hated taking spelling tests. No matter how hard she tried, she couldn't score a high grade. One night her dad suggested he help her study. "Oh, Daddy, nothing will help me," Angela said. "I'm just a terrible speller." Dad insisted they give it a try. Each evening he helped her with the words that might be on the week's test.

Several days after the test, Angela's dad wondered why she had said nothing about how she did. "I didn't want to tell you that I messed up again," she sobbed. "I misspelled five out of twenty words and got a B-."

Dad smiled and said, "I think we should go out for some ice cream and celebrate."

Angela looked puzzled. "What are we celebrating? I didn't get the A that I wanted."

Dad looked into her eyes and said, "We are celebrating you, sweetheart. We are honoring your effort and all of your other skills and talents."

I learned this story shortly after Angela's dad died, long after she had become an accomplished adult. "It was a moment I'll always remember," she told me. What a legacy to leave your child.

Parents often brush their child's cries for validation of their worth aside. They are so focused on their own issues that they forget to appreciate the essence of the child's perceptions. Adults can become so consumed with the pressures of modern living, earning money, and getting their own needs met that they become emotionally or physically unavailable. When you forget to connect with your child, you lose a chance to strengthen the security and bonding vital for the healthy feelings that foster confidence, cooperation, and good decision making.

Your true power doesn't come from controlling. It happens when you seize each moment to help your child feel accepted and valued. An unexpected hug, pat on the shoulder, note of appreciation, recognition of effort, time spent together, and giant smile are all ways you cement a bond. These tiny, seemingly insignificant flashes of connectedness are sparks that become the fuel for raising a child with a sense of lovability and worthiness. Kids who feel good are more likely to make wise choices.

AN ERA OF SHIFTING ENERGY

For a long time children were controlled by fear, guilt, and shame. These same children grew into adults who struggled with their childhood wounds and unwittingly passed a chain of pain to their offspring. As a species we are currently participating in one of the most dynamic shifts the human race has ever experienced. More and more parents are embracing the clarity and confidence to move through daily hurdles with a faith in their ability to teach through their own growth, determined to live in their highest potential.

What does this transformative shift look like? Parents are reading books, taking classes and having deep conversations, seeking to understand a new consciousness, willing to replace ego-driven behavior with a soul-driven desire to live a more purposeful life. The children being born today are demanding that we let go of fear based, old-fashioned discipline techniques and create a more authentic way of being with each other.

The question the conscious parent asks is no longer, "How do I get my child to acquiesce, to listen, to conform or to submit passively?" The parent now asks, "How do I encourage the gifts, the sparkle, the possibilities, the magnificence of this child to shine forth?"

The message the authentically powerful parent gives is: "You are worthy of love and belonging, my child. Courage and determination are in your cosmic design. You are a genius creator, capable of thriving, filled with curiosity and ripe for joyful living. All the answers you seek are inside you. I am here to cheer you on and I will support rather than control you as you walk in the direction of your dreams."

As a species, we are shifting in the way we understand children's behavior. Past generations believed it was their responsibility to control children's feelings and actions. We thought our goal was mostly about teaching children how to behave correctly. We now know that children's behavior is fueled by their emotions. Parenting from authentic power means we stop telling them how they "should" feel and encourage them to explore how they actually do feel.

Two of the most important emotional needs of all humans are to feel connected and empowered. Children need to feel connected to other emotionally healthy friends and family members who model kindness, joy, and appreciation for life. Humans also need to feel a healthy sense of self-empowerment. To be empowered is to feel a connection to our center. Consequently it's almost impossible to feel empowered when someone else is controlling us.

Children don't want advice, criticism, or judgment when they share their struggles. They want to trust us to offer empathy and a safe space to work through life's inevitable challenges. Young people need to know that their inner world belongs to them and that if they share the depth of their being, it won't be met with skepticism or suggestions from the very people who can't seem to get their own acts together. Open communication begins with a willingness to let down our defensive need to be 'right.' As parents expand our own awareness we intuitively open up to a deeper knowing of how to handle challenges that created suffering for previous generations.

We currently live in a society that struggles with pretense and heartache. If we truly want to leave a better world to our children it isn't just the economy or global warming that needs our attention. What happens in the privacy of our homes needs to change. It is time to give up trying to control the uncontrollable, relinquishing power 'over' our children, abandoning the illusions of success, so that we discover where our authentic power lies. The children being born are bringing with them a huge capacity for love and compassion. Many of them won't tolerate the inauthentic, hypocritical, manipulative parenting styles that seemed to work for past generations. They are insisting on change.

A child who grows up in a home in which their cosmic design is understood and respected, their fundamental needs are met, and their parents work on being true to their authentic center, is a child who has a greater potential for mastering the art of feeling good and manifesting well-being no matter what else is happening around them.

More than anything, children of all ages just want their parents to be less stressed and authentically happy. While toys, gadgets and clothes have always been on their 'bucket lists,' many kids would trade in the latest electronic invention to live in a home that is emotionally stable, supportive and nurturing.

Give yourself permission to slow down, get off your technological devices, give up being perfect, and spend more time giving hugs and messages of appreciation. Unconditional love is forgiving, nonjudgmental, sees beyond behavior as it holds a silent space that illuminates the vision of our loved ones fulfilling their destiny.

You can do this. You and your children deserve to know what magnificent creatures you are. Release any urge to control and watch the magic begin.

You now know the most powerful secrets of parenting: no mater what your child experiences, no matter what your child says or does, you can and must maintain your own state of well-being. Your happiness does not depend on someone else changing. Consequently, you are free to love your children exactly as they are and be a powerful influence in modeling how to live an authentically inspired life.

10 BEST PRACTICES FOR PARENTS

These are most effective when you commit to an ongoing process of self-reflection. In order to stay conscious and aware of your inner dialogue it will be incredibly helpful to also put these in writing and to share your insights with your parenting partner. This is an on going process that is done from a place of love, acceptance and non-judgment.

1. Create a vision statement of the ideals and standards you want to model and live with your children. You risk becoming a hypocrite if you are not willing to live in your highest integrity. You cannot control their journey but you can be an inspiring influence.

2. Stay aware of your childhood story, unconscious wounds and ingrained beliefs because they impact parenting decisions.

3. Move past your ego and name the doubts, fears, and judgments that you would like to clean up so they do not trigger your reactivity.

4. Practice reframing the way you interpret your daily experiences. Be courageous in releasing control and breaking the cycle of limiting thinking that has become your Truth.

5. See the world through your children's temperament, stages of development and emotional maturity. Do not demand them to experience the world through your eyes. Give them your full, adoring attention.

6. Observe and reflect on how well your home environment offers consistent, predictable routines and expectations. Be mindful of building relationships of safety and compassion, where young and old are free to voice opinions, learn from misjudgments, and appreciate the uniqueness of each family member.

7. Remember that behavior is always indicative of how well needs are being met. Instead of interpreting misbehavior as a personal affront, use it to wonder about your child's inner world. Seek professional support when adult or children's reactions become extreme.

8. Learn emotionally healthy strategies to promote responsibility and self-control. Fear and punishment never serve authentic learning. They merely create an illusion of cooperation. Provide opportunities for children to experience personal empowerment within a structure of clear, age appropriate expectations and limits.

9. Talk to your children about your own emotional responses, what you are thinking and how it makes you feel. Let them know that how you perceive and interpret things can be shifted. The willingness and determination to change beliefs and habits is the bedrock of personal power. Apologizing for poor behavior and the willingness to do it differently the next time is a sign of strength, not weakness.

10. Cultivate family rituals and habits that encourage open dialogue, freedom to disagree and appreciation of life exactly as it is. Seeing the good in every challenge supports resiliency and learning to tune in to their spiritual essence helps children connect with inner guidance. When the issues of the day seem to clog up the flow of love, remind yourself that nothing is worth the suffering that comes from holding on to worry or anger.

Above all, allow your love to sparkle. Children grow quickly and before you know it, the house will be quiet and clean because they will be off on a journey beyond your control.

You will miss them being close, so savor the years you do have together.

Lighten up and enjoy the ride. Ultimately we are all made of stardust.

Sandi Schwartz received her Masters Degree in Child Development and Education from Columbia University. She is an internationally recognized educator, author, inspirational speaker and parent coach. She has developed a method of understanding and responding to children that transforms unwanted behavior into cooperation and encourages their best to emerge as they grow into compassionate, responsible citizens of the world.

The Schwartz Method© was developed from 40 years of working directly with children as well as training, supervising and mentoring educators. Sandi's certification workshops have been taught to parents from around the world. Her online class, college programs and international radio show have helped adults understand the inner world of children while finding their own authentic power to cultivate emotionally healthy relationships.

Sandi founded Leading Edge Parenting, LLC after receiving accolades from Wall Street executives and recognition from the Governor of New York. Acknowledging that balancing a busy life can create stress for even the most successful and loving adults, she remains dedicated to supporting today's parents in their desire to raise children into their highest integrity.

Sandi serves as CEO of Leading Edge Parenting and offers compassionate and humorous seminars, talks and private consulting to parents, grandparents, organizations, public and private schools, directors and administrators.

For more information visit www.LeadingEdgeParenting.com

After enjoying a successful career as a professional photographer Melissa Schwartz joined Leading Edge Parenting as Creative Director. It was when her mom began writing *Authentic Parenting Power*, that they started talking about the challenges of Melissa's childhood. What Sandi experienced as stubborn, Melissa experienced as self-empowerment. What was perceived as over-reactive, felt to Melissa, perfectly normal. These soulful conversations made them realize how disconnections are created when adults misinterpret

children's behavior. Melissa's ability to articulate what it was like to be a challenging child transformed Sandi's theories into practical wisdom.

Melissa always knew that she would be an advocate for children. While building her photography business Melissa became a nanny. Using her mom as a professional coach, they began developing a system of understanding and responding to children's authentic needs. Melissa transferred the wisdom that made her a beloved caregiver into her work as a photojournalist. The ability to cultivate a safe environment, a willingness to engage the child's inner world and her desire to be a source of unconditional love resulted in authentic, emotional portraits.

In seeing the transformational power of The Schwartz Method©, Melissa made the decision to shift the focus of her life's work to spreading this wisdom. Bringing fifteen years of practical experience with children from infancy through teenagers, into her work, she has earned a reputation as someone who truly understands how to 'be' with children. She now coaches nannies in how to recognize the unmet needs that drive misbehavior and offers strategies that inspire cooperation and positive responses without guilt, threats, shame or punishment. Melissa's greatest passion is sharing this wisdom with nannies wanting to deepen their understanding and take their skills and strengths to a higher level.

For more information, visit www.MelissaSchwartz.com

Made in the USA
Charleston, SC
14 April 2014